YOU TOO CAN LIVE VERY LONG

AL TWOSTONES

VO P&P

Copyright © 2023 by Al Twostones

All rights reserved.

No part of this book may be reproduced in any form or by any electronic or mechanical means, including information storage and retrieval systems, without written permission from the publisher, except for the use of brief quotations in a book review.

Cover design by Arjan van Woensel

Published by VO Productions & Publishing

post@vo-pp.com

For me, someday

Irony is the hygiene of the mind.

Elizabeth Bibesco

Part I

INTRODUCTION

Chapter One

I wonder, dear reader, how you came to be reading this book. Either it's pure coincidence, or someone recommended it to you, or maybe—and this would definitely be my preferred option—it has already gained some popularity among people. Unless it was the title that lured you. Quite a tempting prospect, isn't it? Whatever the reason, I'm really happy you're reading my book because it means that I've managed to finish it. This is not that obvious at the current stage of production, with ninety-five words so far (including "with ninety-five words so far"). It also means that I found a publisher for it, which is even less obvious. If I've been looking for one at all. Enticed by the prospect of making more money, I could have published it myself.

This book tells no story, either made-up or true. So if light, easily digestible prose is your thing, you might want to consider reading something else. The same goes for anyone looking for quick and easy ways to attain inner harmony, get ahead in business, shed excess pounds, or master three languages in five weeks (or five languages in three weeks)—whether selectively or all at once—with success assured and no effort required. Well, this text might be of some assistance in finding inner peace, but the process isn't going to be a quick or effortless one. And to the readers who misinterpreted the title, let me tell you right away: this is not a health guide either. Consider yourself warned. I mention all this because every prudent author, before reaching for a pen (or rather for a keyboard), needs to think about the prospective readership. The broader the target, the smaller the risk of missing it—with or without a publisher.

After many conversations in which I indicated what I was going to write about (in a veiled way, of course, camouflaging myself as a potential author), I gained the impression that the topic might be of interest to quite a few people. Not bad so far. On the other hand, consuming the content of this book, not to mention digesting it, requires some intellectual effort that not everyone might be willing to make. Some might even not be able to. We need to bear in mind that a large proportion of *Homo sapiens* representatives are still at a relatively early stage of development. This is perfectly understandable given the time we've had at our disposal. One way or another, the desired broad target can shrink significantly.

Although, perversely, it doesn't have to be that way. In the seclusion of our minds, the majority of us like to count ourselves as the elite minority able to reason quite efficiently. There is some contradiction here because the majority cannot be a minority, but from a personal perspective everything seems okay. So dedicating this book to the intellectual cream may prove a clever marketing strategy. I dedicate then, since I consider myself a reasonable author. Let's do a quick poll now... Bingo! The number of potential readers is heading north again!

An important factor in the success of a book is the author himself. Unfortunately, at least at first glance, the situation here doesn't appear to be very promising. I cannot boast a particularly rich writing or scientific output. To be perfectly frank, I cannot boast any output. I would like to point out that this is only true of larger literary forms. I regularly do shorter ones, such as emails or text messages. Of course, one could idealistically assume that what is written is more important than who wrote it, but in practice it doesn't work very well.

To raise my status as an author, let's provisionally assume that I am the incarnation of Albert Einstein. I have compelling evidence that I am. Reading his famous sayings, I was amazed by how closely they match my own thoughts. Did I get a little too far about that Einstein scenario? Well, with some luck, it's not entirely out of the question. Besides, this isn't my idea. About two thousand years ago someone already suggested that the last will be the first and vice versa. I'm going to defend this proposal anyway, albeit from a slightly different position.

There is one more thing to consider. Why should I write this book at all? To make the world a better place? Just kidding; I barely manage to keep my own mental and physical state in check. Besides, global saviors—and local ones too—are a pretty shady bunch of people, occasionally even dangerous. I don't mean their intentions, which may be noble at times (though they don't necessarily have to be). I am referring to the consequences of their missionary work. In order to make others happy, they propose universal solutions, even though a cursory observation reveals that everyone has different preferences.

Personal fame, or even a minor popularity, doesn't appeal to me either. By gaining one or another, you need to have the potential not to derail. I'm not sure I possess a sufficient quantity of it. Once, quite accidentally, I got my room upgraded at a hotel. The new one was located on the top floor, following the rule that the further from the ground, the higher the standard... and the price, of course. On the second day of my stay, I discovered that I enjoy pressing the top button in the hotel elevator. I enjoyed it even more when other passengers, who then got off on the lower floors, observed it. I'm not even sure if they knew the floor hierarchy.

Okay, let's say the motive is to share an idea that simply answers some of the questions that have occupied people's minds since the dawn of time. Why do we live? What's the point of it all? And a few other thoughts that may be useful in everyone's lives (plural intentional). On the other hand, how do you know I'm not talking nonsense? What does it matter that I myself am convinced of something? It's easy to mess with people's heads, especially if there are no consequences. So, being aware of my responsibilities as a writer, I hereby change my motivation. From here on I write just for myself. Should you decide to continue reading, you do so at your own risk.

I also write for myself for purely selfish reasons. I'm not sure if I'll be able to retrieve my current knowledge in the future. I think I will, but you know how the saying goes—better safe than sorry. If this book happens to be popular, there is a good chance I will stumble upon it somehow. Then I'll only have to read it and maybe even ponder a little over its content. You, dear reader, also have a choice. A free choice. Don't let some wise guys fool you into thinking that free will is an illusion. It is the essence of human existence. Of all the living creatures, only we benefit from this boon, so don't miss the opportunity, even if it does involve effort, risks, and occasional side effects.

If this book becomes popular, I won't despise a certain financial bonus resulting from that popularity. I am fully aware that the possession of surplus money invites various risks, such as burglary, ransom kidnapping, or—in the event that no third party is involved—possible destruction, usually mental, of the surplus holder. I will consider it, say, as an interesting experiment to what extent I'm going to be susceptible (or immune) to this destruction. And you, dear reader, can support me in this study. Recommend this book to your family or friends. Or buy another copy for them yourself—they have birthdays and celebrate Christmas, don't they?

Chapter Two

Researchers of all kinds of things and phenomena—in the old days, the ignorant mob called jugglers and charlatans, and today, after gaining universal respect, named scientists—describe their achievements in a rather convoluted way. The average man in the street doesn't understand most of it. Maybe that's the point? Sometimes I even get the impression that the researchers themselves don't really know what they're talking about. But there's no one out there who is able to check.

Once, stubbornly tracing the essence of quantum mechanics, I stumbled across a short video that promised to provide a sixth-grade-level explanation. Hurray, I thought, filled with hope. Finally, I was going to understand something about the topic. Not this time. It was the same linguistic and conceptual mishmash additionally ornamented with poor-quality illustrations. Taking a critical look at my own mental performance, I provisionally assumed that maybe I was the problem here. Sometime later, I listened to a famous mathematical physicist (he even won the Nobel Prize recently) speaking on the topic. He expressed quite a few reservations and doubts himself—this time in a clear and comprehensible way. I calmed down a bit.

This book is written in such a way that any willing reader

should be capable of absorbing it. That was the plan, anyway. You may not agree with my ideas, but you should be able to understand them (provided you make some effort). Because of the subject, it can probably be classified as somewhat of a philosophical work—without ambition for any scientific recognition. (I rhyme a little, but the rhythm—have mercy, Lord!) As an author, I am in no way an educated thinker. Nor do I have any academic titles or publications in wise journals. So you may doubt that I'm qualified enough to speak on such serious matters.

And what about Socrates? After all, he was the greatest philosopher of all time, or at least one of the greatest. I found no mention of his academic education (he was said to be a brave and valiant warrior instead). He wasn't in the habit of documenting his ideas on paper either (or parchment, to be precise). So, dear doubters, I am in really good company. Besides, I wouldn't be penning this book if I knew someone else would do it for me. Putting thoughts on paper is a tedious and exhausting task. On the other hand, it helps you develop a great deal, so maybe I would write it anyway.

I might also add that my spiritual ancestor Albert used to say: "Imagination is more important than knowledge." (I want to remind you that this ancestor business is just marketing.) To claim, for example, that the Earth is round and not flat—as was once commonly believed—you didn't have to be a great or even a minor scholar, or a sailor circumnavigating it. Simple logic suggested that there was no other option. The problem is that simplicity and logic don't enjoy any immense popularity, and nothing has changed here for quite a long time. Something even tells me that the previous sentence won't need to be updated in future editions of this book, whether they appear in five, five hundred, or five thousand years (if they appear at all).

Even to this day you can easily stumble upon people claiming in all seriousness that the Earth is flat. There's nothing unusual about that. Since the dawn of time, people with admirable zeal have been engaged in inventing various stories, even quite ridiculous ones. This tradition is still alive and well. The flat-Earth concept is no exception, and given its rather limited number of followers, it remains nothing but a funny quirk. Things get much worse when too many people start believing in a fairy tale. Sometimes, we all do. So perhaps instead of mocking flat-earthers and offering them your pity (even if it makes you feel better), spare a moment every now and then and take a critical look at your own views. While this option requires a bit of effort and self-criticism, it's far more useful for one's own development.

An attentive reader will probably notice that I tend to generalize and simplify in this book. This is not due to incompetence or laziness but was a well-considered decision. There is no need to dig into details if it doesn't matter much for the so-called big picture. On top of that, it may discourage further reading, and I'm not going to shoot myself in the foot. It's like pestering travelers with information about the technological processes required for the train to stop at a station (and after a short while leave again). From the passenger's point of view, this is irrelevant. His rail vehicle only needs to continue, preferably in the right direction, and reach its destination on time.

The same observant reader (or maybe a different one) might detect, by contrast, that I keep dealing with some issues, compulsively repeating the arguments for or against. This may lead to a certain impatience on the part of the readership or, God forbid, an underestimation of the author's literary skills. Let me explain—this, too, is intentional. (I decidedly dispel the rumors of the early symptoms of dementia.) I can't just rely on a savvy audience. If you catch on quickly or have a good memory, you can always skip this or that paragraph. Or take a break—get some coffee or stretch your legs for a couple of minutes.

Using the proven method of the aforementioned Socrates, I'm going to ask questions. The difference is, I won't bother other people, just myself. Inquisitive questioning of outsiders forces them to formulate answers. This effort might not necessarily be justified from their point of view. After a short time, it may even be perceived as an attempt at harassment. If they nonetheless decide to make the effort, it may reveal the superficiality of their judgments, or even expose their incompetence. And this is something people generally dislike. Oh, they do! In the case of Socrates, this resulted in his slightly premature travel to the Other Side (although not without the collaboration of the participant himself). Keeping this fact in mind, I will only harass myself. Given that the bully and the victim is the same person, a similar unpleasant ending is rather unlikely.

The first question I'm going to ask myself is: What do we live for? I know, I know, I fired the cannons right away. Don't worry, the answer is not that complicated. If you look closely at processes run by Nature and realize that humans are part of it, we live to evolve. In addition, everyone should focus on their own development and not disturb others by pursuing the same goal.

Actually, that's all I have to say. At this point I could basically finish the writing. (Maybe still add THE END below.) On the other hand, two chapters might be a bit too hard to sell as a book. I also have the feeling that a part of the readers would expect some clarification of this, I must admit, rather vaguely formulated statement. Well, it looks like I have no choice but to keep writing.

Part II

HOW NATURE WORKS

Chapter Three

How is it that the world around us creates such perfect conditions for life to thrive? Some say it's dumb luck. Others believe that it would be impossible to tune all the necessary elements so precisely without some kind of creative touch. In my opinion, both claims are wrong.

To see this, all you have to do is take a good look at how Nature works. No, not the one we like to spend time in, with flowers in the meadow, birds chirping, and lions ripping their prey to shreds. I mean the all-powerful one, spelled with a capital N, that is everywhere and runs everything. As soon as you do, you will inevitably conclude that it works in an absolutely perfect and yet incredibly simple way.

The driving force behind all processes occurring in Nature is the urge to evolve. This is done through ongoing interactions. As a result, new structures emerge. They are constantly verified and then improved or destroyed if they are deemed unsustainable. The subsequent interactions create new, more resistant, durable, and advanced structures, which are verified again. This process goes on and on, endlessly. The structures may be physical or other; the principle remains the same.

Such a process, although very time consuming, is the only way to achieve the best possible result at any given time and continue optimal development. By "time consuming" I mean from the perspective of the human being. From Nature's point of view, time doesn't matter. Or to put it another way, Nature has an infinite amount of time at its disposal. Whether something lasts an hour or millions of years is irrelevant. The process described above affects everything: a non-living matter, a living one, and its particularly advanced form, humans.

Please stop reading for a moment. Wait, that's a slightly irrational suggestion since if you don't continue, you won't know why. Well, then carry on—but don't rush. Because I'm about to run a test right now. If you are reading an e-book, mark the current page and switch the device off. You have a paperback? Just close it and put it away. You might want to memorize the page number or grab a bookmark. Ready? By the way, I wonder how you are going to read now. Anyway, let's not nitpick, I'm sure you'll think of something. Now tell me (or rather yourself) what you remember from the previous three paragraphs. No peeking, please! This is a serious scientific experiment!

If you haven't memorized much, I suggest rereading. For those who have trouble counting or don't know what a paragraph is, start with: "To see this, all you have to do is take a good look at how Nature works." Besides, this statement will help you understand many different phenomena and events. Since you are here, I presume you've learned your material now. Just to be sure—as a prudent author I have to take care of all my readers, including those prone to laziness—you can find the abridged version below. You have a bad memory? Don't worry, I will repeat it in this book from time to time.

The driving force behind all processes occurring in Nature is the urge to evolve. It is an ongoing process of interactions and verifications. It creates new structures, improves existing ones, or destroys them if the checks fail. This scheme guarantees the best possible outcome and further optimal development. It concerns every form of matter, as well as humans.

Right, matter. Everything that surrounds or fills us is made up of small particles of matter. They are connected in different ways. Depending on the stage at which it appeared, how it changed or evolved, and the level of advancement, we can divide it into three main categories: non-living matter, living matter, and humans. Biologically, humans are, no doubt, part of living matter. Still, I separate us from bacteria, grass, or even chimpanzees. In the same way, I distinguish bacteria, grass, and chimpanzees from stone, shovel, or car—in spite of the fact that these nice organisms consist of particles of matter. Although since a car moves from time to time, it could be considered more advanced than grass. It is even faster than a chimpanzee.

In Nature there are also fixed and powerful forces. They are there for matter (not only) to evolve. It's like a game of chess. All the pieces moving on the chessboard are particles or larger structures of matter. Natural forces define how they behave and interact. The pawn moves forward, never retreats, and captures or checks diagonally. The bishop also captures and checks diagonally but in both directions, and it moves as far as it wants. The knight jumps, captures, and checks in all directions but in a rather chaotic way. As for the rook and the royal couple, I'm running out of time, so please check guides instead. Without these rules, if the moves were completely random, the game of chess would make no sense (except for the numb rearrangement of pieces on the board). In Nature, forces make the rules, and the game takes place without players and their interference—another rule for this game to have meaning and purpose.

Researchers currently speak of four fundamental forces. These include gravity, electromagnetism, and two nuclear ones: weak and, by contrast, strong. Some others bind atoms and molecules. They have less-exciting names, so I won't bother listing them. All these forces played a key role in the development of non-living matter. Then two more came to the fore. The first supported the transition from non-living to living matter and the fantastic growth of the latter. The other played the same role at the interface between organisms and humans.

Scholars remain silent about the last two forces, but I do not.

They are silent because they haven't met them yet. For me, it's enough that I am able to imagine them. Or let's say, I can't imagine how everything would work without them. It's a simple logic I follow, similar to assuming a round, rather than flat, Earth. And just to be clear, when I talk about the power that enables life to arise and evolve, I don't mean Helmont's "Vis Vitalis," Bergson's "Elan Vital," nor is it "Prana," "Qi" or whatever. You have no idea what I'm talking about? That's all right. You can remain in a state of blissful ignorance. Nothing dramatic is going to happen in your life because of it.

Let me make it even clearer. Just because a certain set of ingredients in a favorable environment initiates the processes of life, that doesn't answer the most basic of all questions: Why? What enables these ingredients to do so? An explanation that "that's just the way it is, and, given the right external conditions, they interact or influence each other in a certain beneficial way" is a weak argument. It would be like saying that something attracts something else because both are made up of elements that attract each other, and there are favorable conditions to this attraction. It couldn't be any clearer, at least I've already exhausted my potential.

It's getting a little controversial. There is nothing I can do about it (except stop writing), and this trend is going to manifest itself more and more throughout the book. So, dear reader, especially if you have a strong educational background (and are allergic to laypeople who happen to be insufferable know-it-alls), let me just remind you that my opinions don't aspire, in any way or under any circumstances, to anything. If you want to come at them from an academic point of view, this will prove to be a mare's nest. Or even a jenny's. This of course doesn't mean that I have an aversion to constructive and logical criticism. In fact, it's quite the contrary. If you have the time and energy, then by all means, be skeptical. Just make sure the language is clear so I know what it's all about.

Chapter Four

The least complex form of matter is the non-living one. In the very beginning, a dozen or so billion years ago (if scholars are to be believed), there were single, moving particles of it. Following Nature's trends, they joined together, broke apart, joined again, forming first small and simple, then larger and more advanced, structures. This is how hydrogen, the simplest and most common component in the universe came to be. Next was helium, followed by lithium and others. About this hydrogen and Co business, this is obviously the speculation of researchers but not a particularly crazy one, so let it stay that way.

More inquisitive readers might want me to clarify what I mean by "the very beginning." Well, nothing in particular. I'm quite partial to the suggestion that there was a high-energetic eruption of some quarks or other bosons. What really happened and how is quite irrelevant, and we will probably never know, why should we? It only gets interesting when you start thinking about what was before (take it easy—just to stretch your mind a bit). Some claim there was nothing. Well, even taking into account their academic ranks and achievements, the concept makes no sense at all. If you proclaim that something happened at some point, then another something must also have existed before. You don't need to be a particularly keen thinker to come up with that. And if you don't know what it was, just say "I don't know." This is a much better solution than making up stories, even if they include nothing.

If there was a beginning and something before, the first thing that comes to mind is a cycle. The famous mathematical physicist I mentioned earlier—I like to listen to him because I understand what he is saying (even though he uses a foreign language)—suggested that the conditions at the beginning and the end of our universe should be very similar. That could mean a transition from one into another. I like this idea because it sounds logical. And when I think of a cycle, in my mind's eye I see a circle or a sphere. In two-dimensional reality, something moving around a circle travels the same route over and over again. This something, however, may believe that it is moving steadily forward and pushing into new territories. And nothing can convince it otherwise, unless it pauses and thinks for a moment or two—as long as it is capable of thought, of course.

If there are more than three dimensions (that's all we've gotten familiar with so far), and some multidimensional *circlesphericity* exists... Who knows, maybe everything would suddenly become much simpler. On the other hand, there is no need to dwell on it or even fantasize about it. It's of no use to us whatsoever. By the way, if there was a beginning and something before, then what was before that previous before? There is always something before and something after. Like I said, it goes round and round.

The proponents of the initial explosion call it grandly the Big Bang. (Which makes me irresistibly think of famous Indian chiefs, like Red Cloud, Sitting Bull, or Crazy Horse.) Some suggest that time also started with the explosion. They came up with this idea to justify that there was nothing before, and there will be the same nothing after. I wonder how this time came about? Did it just pop out of some crack? Did it swirl or ripple for a while and then spill all over the place? Or did it squander, maybe?

I dare to offer another definition. Time is a measure invented by humans. A very useful tool, especially in everyday life. It works best when it's limited to a practicable scale. For example, one revolution around the axis or one lap around the sun, plus their reasonable divisions and multiples. Let's say, from a millisecond to a million years. More is just *an awful lot*. In Nature, by contrast, which—if you think about it logically—always had to be and always will be, time is irrelevant. There is no need to pursue the topic further because it adds nothing. Or, if you will, it's a waste of time.

"If you think about it logically." I tend to use the noun "logic," as well as the adjective and adverb derived from it, quite a lot in this book. But I need to be careful. The meaning of this word is not as obvious as I had thought it was. I once listened to an expert who knew the subject. He argued that if we make false assumptions, the results will admittedly be false, but consistent with logic... Or something like that. Let's assume then that six is the correct result of adding two to three. I can now insist that the equation $(2+3) \times 2 = 12$ is logically correct. In math class, that stubbornness would result in getting an F. However, if the numbers teacher was on leave and a philosopher was the substitute, the grade would be much better.

Let us now assume that the lion is a herbivore (a plant-eating animal, in normal language). I am on a trip to Africa and I suddenly see a muscular, broad-chested cat with a prominent mane in front of me. I conclude—logically—that I'm not in danger... It was my last assumption, I guess. And let me clarify: I only try to use a certain kind of logic, which is called common sense. It relies on the assumption (there we go, the next one) that a false result cannot be considered logically correct. Because there is not an ounce of sense in this—common or otherwise.

Dear author, I must here remind you that the subject of this chapter is non-living matter and its evolution... Oh, sure. How did it go? "The process of changes should lead to the best possible result at any given time." Sounds good, but how do you get it in practice?

Rule number one: for something to change or grow, it has to be harassed, vigorously and from all directions. Serious problems must be guaranteed, so that insufficient structures can't cope with them. Rule number two: this process must not be interfered with in any way. Rule number three: very strict quality control and ruthless elimination of duds are essential. Think about a car crash test. You pound the vehicle against the wall and make adjustments until the construction proves strong and safe enough, eliminating the ones that don't hold up. Except with Nature the standards are much more stringent.

The final rule is that the rules can't change. All that remains is to properly calibrate natural forces, and the perfect machinery can start to operate. Small particles of matter harassed each other, attaching themselves to each other from time to time. But even then they couldn't find peace because other particles, single or attached, harassed them as well. Those unable to withstand this harassment detached themselves and began to harass others, which couldn't stand it either, so, already detached, they harassed others, possibly attaching to them. This went on and on, gradually leading to larger and more complex structures of attachment. If we take a time perspective of an awful lot of years, this is how planets, stars, galaxies, and other nebulae or pulsars were formed—as well as some smaller stuff, like moons, comets, meteorites, asteroids, and their various satellites. And there is supposedly a lot of them, not to say an awful lot.

The Earth and its surroundings were born in a similar way. This is hardly a new or controversial hypothesis. The next one, however, has everything it needs to meet the criteria. I claim that it is highly probable, bordering on certainty, that the whole process of transformation of non-living matter was aimed precisely so as to form a place stable enough and located in the right environment for life to emerge and thrive. That was the strategic goal, so to speak. Trials were held all over the place, ending with success on the small sphere orbiting a medium-sized star in our solar system, in a galaxy called the Milky Way.

Which makes our planet quite unique. Are there other places like this in the universe? The occurrence of a similar sequence of events, or any other that would allow life to emerge, is highly unlikely. A statistician would tell you that this is not entirely impossible. So there is still hope for people looking for extraterrestrial civilizations. And that strategic goal was just a part of a much bigger strategy. The formation of Earth was only the first step along the way, albeit an extremely important one. Without it, nothing more could be set in motion. It's like a bricklayer breaking ground so that he can proceed with the construction. I just wonder... how tall? The first and second floor for sure; we already know that.

Part III

LIFE

Chapter Five

How did life originate on Earth? Life processes are just another emanation of Nature's drive for growth, however diametrically different from the previous one. I read the last sentence again and I'm a bit confused. I promised to use simple and understandable language. Do "emanation" and "diametrically" still satisfy the criteria? On the other hand, I somehow like these words. Okay, I'm going to take the risk, and if there's trouble, I'll give an educational motive. I offer some readers a unique opportunity to expand their linguistic resources.

What were the qualities of this diametrically different emanation. Until life appeared, the changes were, shall we say, strictly mechanical. They involved just mixing and building combinations of the available raw material. The matter subjected to these treatments had no creative power, so to speak. Then something absolutely extraordinary happened. The same witless matter suddenly began to replicate itself.

We have to realize how radical of a change this was. Which, by the way, doesn't occur particularly often in Nature. What gave rise to it? Just water and the warm rays of the sun? I have my doubts. Some researchers blame everything on genes, thus confirming that even long-lasting educational training doesn't result in the ability to distinguish cause from effect. This is like someone claiming that a car moves because its wheels spin. The agency of this rotation seems to be less important. I'm going to insist on another natural force initiating and supporting the processes of life. There is no other way to explain such a significant breakthrough in the evolution of matter. Which doesn't change the fact that whether something exists or does not exist doesn't hinge upon what someone thinks about it. Even though that someone spent a lot of time thinking about it.

In the case of life, there's a cycle again—which convinces me all the more that it didn't arise from spontaneous chaos but is subject to the iron rules of a powerful and perfect mechanism. As is always the case in Nature. Something is born, grows, and then dies, only to be reborn and continue to grow. Verily (as the old-fashioned would say), only the cycle really makes sense. In contrast, imagine that biological life has no end. Such a prospect, at least at first glance, would probably please many of us (unless you work in the funeral industry). A second glance, however, would probably leave many people depressed. We could conclude that we don't exist at all. Who would want to make us, and what for?

Even if the mode was different, the principle of how living matter evolved remained the same. The process included ongoing interactions and testing of new structures, now referred to as organisms. Quality was prioritized, while duds ended up in the landfill. A spectacular example that perfectly illustrates this mechanism is the history of dinosaurs. At one point they completely dominated our planet. It may have seemed—both from their perspective and the rest of its inhabitants—that they were absolutely invincible.

All it took to get rid of them was a sufficiently large stone. Or maybe something else; it doesn't really matter. Lulled by their evolutionary success over millions of years, they were verified by Nature and, as defective goods, sent back into oblivion. It's not that hard to guess why this happened—they were simply too big. Other animals that exercised growth restraint survived harsh conditions. Let this be a universal warning against gigantomania and the exaggerated ego. The development of humans is subject to the same principle.

Sooner or later, we too will hear the voice of Nature saying "Call." And if we were bluffing, we need to get ready for a serious drop in our holdings. We can only hope that we didn't play "all-in."

Life, of course, didn't emerge in a single, perceptible moment. It took a long time between the first more-or-less random impulse—where a certain undefined, microscopic, yet already sufficiently advanced bit of non-living matter found the right environment and turned out to be susceptible to the influence of the all-powerful but so far poorly utilized life force—and the first self-replication process.

I took a glance at what I just wrote. I am not sure whether a sentence with fifty-seven words and eight punctuation marks between them is a testament to literary finesse or rather to its absence. Fearing the second, I thought of a reedit of sorts. I looked at my watch, the hour was quite late... Wait a minute! How about engaging the consumers a bit more? And attaching them stronger to the product? Dear reader! If you have a good idea about how to make it better (no, not the world, just this sentence), I look forward to your suggestions. I'll include the best one in the next edition of this book.

So, a lot of time has passed. Nature doesn't tolerate sloppiness, and considering what was about to happen, some really decent preparations were required. For the first time, matter was given the ability to make decisions. Initially it was more an illusion. Over time, gradually, it began to play an increasingly important role. The color of the flowers in a meadow is not really a result of a deliberate choice made by poppies and cornflowers. But the decision of the giraffe's progenitors to put forth some effort and try to reach for higher-growing foliage already contained the element of choice. Of course, it wasn't inspired by some meticulous consideration of all the pros and cons. Their instincts told them what to do to have a better chance of survival.

Speaking of which: Once, lying in the meadow, I wondered why flowers have different colors. Applying an uncomplicated way of thinking, you could assume that, say, the first flower was yellow, the next one (seeing this) chose blue, another one went with red, the next one with pink, and so on. Despite the undeniable charm and simplicity of such a solution, some inner voice told me that this was not the case. I sank into my thoughts. I have to admit that it took me an unexpectedly long time to find a satisfactory answer (thankfully, the weather played along). I'm not going to give it away. Instead, I'd like to encourage you, dear reader, to try and solve this riddle yourself.

Chapter Six

Opportunities like this don't come along every day. After discovering that self-driven activity was within its reach, living matter started to practice it eagerly. At first slowly and carefully and then with ever-greater vigor. This resulted in simple, less simple, and finally quite complex organisms of all sorts that took over water, land, and air. I read somewhere that the number is estimated at 8 to 8.7 million species. The vast majority have yet to be described, which is going to take more than a thousand years. I like the ease with which scholars deal with numbers, especially if they have many zeros. Another author didn't rule out even a billion different organisms. That would extend the time to catalogue them all into infinity. I have a better suggestion. How about we leave the living things alone? And transfer the funds elsewhere? On the other hand, counting beetles is generally a harmless activity, even if completely unproductive.

A large accumulation of living beings is not particularly surprising. They were mostly engaged in producing offspring, which then did the same. Two methods of this activity were particularly favored. Asexual reproduction is the duplication of oneself. In this variant, the offspring is essentially identical to the parent. The more popular sexual reproduction requires two willing participants, usually a male and a female. The offspring inherits half of their biological assets from each parent.

I recently read that some clever experimentalists decided to outsmart Nature. Or rather just make it better—let's not assume bad intentions right away. They came up with the idea to produce offspring by mating individuals of the same sex. Well, just like in other communities, there will always be a few crazies among professional scholars. Maybe even more in this group. I don't know if this has any meaning—let's take it more symbolically—but even at the level of elementary particles, those with the same charge usually repel one another.

Procreation was typically preceded by accompanying activities. These included puffing up, ruffling feathers or fur (whatever they had), as well as competing in sports. Running, wrestling, and other forms of hand-to-hand (or tooth-to-tooth) combat were particularly popular. Talented participants took part in singing competitions, and the rest just made different noises, sometimes less friendly, sometimes more—depending on whether you wanted to scare or attract your counterpart.

The remaining time was devoted mainly to consumption. There were two streams of this activity to be distinguished. One encompassed all the efforts to eat something or someone. The other was all about not getting eaten. So there was a significant conflict of interest, combined with a strong determination to emerge from this contest full or whole (depending on which side you are rooting for). In spite of the wide variety of potential delicacies, consumption was not driven by a desire to satisfy the demanding palates of consumers. The reason was more economic in nature, so to speak. The victim was simply an energy source.

Right, energy. Until now, I haven't really paid it a lot of attention. As a matter of fact, I've intentionally not even mentioned it once. The topic is a seemingly simple and yet somewhat slippery one. I mean, what is energy? "A scalar quantity describing various processes and interactions occurring in Nature." Oh boy, I truly love this language. And all kinds of scalar quantities as well. "Energy is a property that must be transferred to perform work," I read in another source. This already sounds a bit better, although still quite enigmatic—that's what Grouchy Smurf would probably say.

Even my great ancestor Albert didn't offer a specific definition (at least not one I could find). He spoke only of an equivalent ratio of mass and energy, and that one is a form of the other—if I understood him correctly. He also mentioned that the amount of energy is constant, takes different forms, and cannot be added or subtracted. Okay, using common sense, I see it this way: In the beginning, a certain amount of energy set in motion a certain amount of matter, and this process goes on in different configurations to this day (and will go on for a while). Sure, let's roll with that. I don't need any more sophisticated concepts.

"Energy supports the growth and development of organisms." Oh, that means roughly... everything. No wonder releasing it by consumption has been so popular, especially among more mobile species. Flora, which had a lower demand for energy (as a result of not moving and its simplified design), focused mainly on sustainable use of sunlight, which is in vogue even these days. The rest required more energy, so they fought a fierce battle for access to its sources. Not only with the competition—in the case of predators, also with the sources themselves.

Regardless of their culinary preferences, both vegetarians and individuals that preferred a piece of meat had to keep their bodies in shape. This wasn't dictated by current fads or some common nutritional awareness. It was more about the fact that if you were overweight, you would have a problem getting something to eat and none getting eaten. So if you are planning to shed a few pounds, a method proven for centuries—less food, more exercise—might be worth considering.

The more careful among the readers will by now probably start accusing me of being inconsistent. After all, I warned you that this book doesn't offer weight-loss advice. I strongly oppose this accusation. What I just described is an ancient method that is not grounded in any serious scientific research. It isn't on the list of numerous advisers specializing in digestion, metabolic disorders, or excess cholesterol either. I take no responsibility for the side effects and possible complications caused by the reckless use of this outdated method. I'd still get an adequate insurance plan—just in case.

Homines sapientes (the plural of *Homo sapiens*) are not really afraid that something is going to eat them. So from time to time, or ever so often, they eat too much. Especially the more affluent specimen. People may also eat too little. Children with overprotective parents specialize in this approach. Their desperate guardians subject them to various procedures such as begging, threats, distraction, and even bribery, just to get them to absorb any food. Are we dealing with potential hunger suicides? To see who is soft in the head, parents or offspring, I suggest a simple experiment. It is about the consistent and complete cessation of food for, say, one day. A little fast never hurt anybody, and the child, at first taken aback by such a turn of events, will quickly start demanding any nourishment. The question is, dear parent of a non-eater, whether your kid is going to get this chance at all. It's your choice and your will. Free will. Just keep in mind, it affects another human being, so the responsibility is much higher.

Chapter Seven

The developmental process of organisms on Earth is referred to as evolution. The word "evolution" itself means a gradual, harmonious transformation. (The opposite is a revolution, where changes are rapid and generally fucked-up.) I think evolution would fit nicely as a universal term for all transformations occurring in Nature. I use it quite often in this context. Unfortunately, I'm about 150 years too late with the idea. That is when the term evolution was trademarked and reserved exclusively for the development of earthly living beings, animals in particular.

Today, Evolution (let's write it with a capital E) is a global brand that enjoys a high level of recognition. Something like Coca-Cola, McDonald's, or Google (they don't give me money for sneaky advertising). Most people, when asked who was the inventor and what it's all about will easily point to Darwin and man coming from a monkey. This is, of course, a slightly simplified version of the thoughts of the famous English biologist. You can find more details in his book *On the Origin of Species*, which outlines the mechanisms of natural selection and what that means for these species. I haven't read Darwin's book, but I don't worry about it too much.

His hypotheses, which are easily found elsewhere, are roughly correct. However, there are some issues that concern me, mainly the claim that some species survived while other didn't because Evolution favored it that way, or that some changes were beneficial from Evolution's point of view and therefore happened automatically. This way of framing the question further proves that conceptual mess is alive and well, just like mixing up causes and effects. (I have no idea if it was Darwin himself or some editors who were tinkering with his theory, and I won't know this until I review the source material, which I'm not going to do because the book has too many pages.)

Evolution, even when capitalized, has no creative power. Nor is it about any specific events that cause the changes. It's their description, not the source. Take flowers in a meadow. (Oh yeah, dear reader, you've jumped to the right conclusion. The riddle from a few pages back will now be solved. You were just about to find the answer yourself? Too late, I guess. You just wasted a chance at growth! At the very least, let this serve as a warning so you don't make the same mistake the next time.) The color of the flowers in a meadow was completely random at first. I have no idea what influenced it—some chemical processes or conditions? Doesn't matter. It was also random how many flowers initially chose the same color. Maybe most of them were yellow, fewer were red, and a few more were blue? But still less violet and more orange? Or the other way around? As for the smell and shape, similar chaotic conditions prevailed. Many flowers have tried; only the most attractive (from the point of view of collaborating insects) survived. Nothing controlled it or saw any advantage in anything. The brilliant principle of optimal development—interaction, verification, destruction of poor quality—was enough. The process runs itself and requires no intervention.

The same goes for ants. Evolution didn't come out and tell them they were best in the swarm. The ants didn't know which strategy would prove successful. (How were they supposed to know?) They tested different variants. Those who preferred sticking together, a method that must have had many variations anyway, survived. After all, this didn't take place in a vacuum. Many factors are involved in this process. Where is the anthill, what or whom do we eat, who eats us, how do we procreate? And a swarm of others.

And the anteater didn't have a long and narrow snout because Evolution liked it that way. This was solely due to its persistent attempts to eat the aforementioned ants. Not only did it elongate its mouth, but it made the saliva stickier. With time, it also said goodbye to its teeth, superfluous for eating insects, well in line with the "use it or lose it" principle. And decent claws in the optimal combination of 3+1, extremely useful for rummaging through anthills, were the deserved reward for its effort and perseverance.

Did the anteater have to work so hard? In theory, it could have relaxed and tried eating something more readily available. It was, however, an illusory choice. Lying tongue out and waiting for a flying ant (or at least an ordinary fly) to land on it—which would have to happen quite frequently—ensured a fairly certain death. In the slower version, of starvation. In a faster one, satisfying another's hunger, should a famished lion be marauding in the area.

Not that this could ever happen—they live in different geographic areas. Have I managed to fool you too, dear reader? I would recommend being vigilant when you read, listen, or watch something. I've already told you—people indulge in making up stories with admirable passion. Sometimes there is a confrontation and one tale replaces another. When the theory of Evolution started throwing its weight around the world in the mid-nineteenth century, it wasn't received very warmly by those who thought that the squirrel, hyena, and of course the human were designed and whittled by the omnipotent being they called God. For their part, the ardent apologists of Evolution were rather skeptical of the existence of a divine being, describing religious beliefs as superstition and mental retreat. However, while attributing creative abilities to Evolution, they failed to notice that they had simply switched the omnipotent powers around. One Almighty Creator was replaced by another that removed some living beings and kept others as it pleased.

The anteater's bizarre appearance—in a beauty contest it would place very remotely—wasn't the work of Evolution. It was its own achievement, resulting from constant attempts to catch ants or other termites. The motive was not a thoughtful decision but a simple alternative: either I get fed or someone else does at my expense. Abstract thinking, free will, and choice are tools that are only available to humans. Not that we are able to use them without fuss.

Sometimes, however, there are suggestions that animals can reason, too. I once listened to a discussion where a speaker presented the example of some wild African dogs. Chasing potential dinner, they split into two groups. Some hunters push the prey toward their colleagues, who lurk in the bushes. They jump out at the right moment and perform the killing... something to that effect. The subtext of the statement was clear: there must be a bit more behind such a clever strategy than simple hunting instinct or ordinary hunger. I'm going to follow up on this trail, simultaneously activating my imagination. I see a picture of a secret meeting of African dog commanders. The top dog showcases a psychological portrait of the prey, along with its motor parameters, weather forecast, and topographical plans of the terrain. Finally, various methods for catching the prey are carefully considered and negotiated.

I really appreciate this imagery, but something tells me that the reality is far more mundane. Let's resort to simple math. Suppose it took the African canines a hundred thousand years to test the most effective strategy for obtaining food. This is not a particularly long time in the evolutionary process of any species. Hunger occurs quite frequently, ditto for a closely related eating. Assuming a conservative frequency—once every two to three days—this gives us about fifteen million training units. (Excluding February 29 in leap years.) The conclusion is simple: practice makes perfect, even if it's mindless.

Dear author, do you hold a degree on the topic? So how about humbling yourself and just listening to the experts? Of course animals use their intelligence. They also have the ability to make well-considered choices. That's not all. The same can be said about mushrooms and even trees. I kid you not. This is what some researchers claim. They must know what they're talking about because they've studied these issues for a long time. So it looks like we are not that different from animals. Okay, maybe we are a bit smarter. Maybe we even have a slightly more capable mind. Sure. Whatever. If we spent our holidays with a herd of gorillas, or carefully observing a termite mound, we would easily discover that we have more in common than we thought we did.

I recently read an interview with a rookie scholar (let's go easy on him, given his young age). His research focuses on fungi. I learned that they make decisions and solve problems—and not just the trivial ones. We could learn a lot from them. He mentioned in passing that he occasionally absorbs the hallucinogens produced by the mushrooms himself (as part of his experiments, of course). I consider this, along with his young age, to be a serious mitigating circumstance.

I'm not sure if it was him, or some other virtuoso in the field, who shared this bloodcurdling story. One particularly clever fungus lodges itself inside a beetle. It then animates the insect to climb a tree. After reaching the appropriate altitude, it causes an internal explosion of the host, catapulting the aggressor to its desired location. Not bad, huh? This is what the perfect crime looks like. If I were the head of some informal organization specializing in the traceless elimination of individuals, I would make every effort to keep such a smart cookie on the payroll. Or at least have the occasional collaboration. If the author of the mushroom story took it seriously, I have a suspicion. The same fungus, possibly its confidant, has lodged inside him, secreting some heavily psychedelic extracts.

Chapter Eight

Whatever the cause, the bug has fallen. Which means, its life has come to an end. All living organisms will face the same destiny, although not necessarily under such dramatic circumstances. Death is an inseparable and unavoidable attribute of life. The question is, why did Nature do this to us? Let's compare living beings with those that don't show signs of life. The fact that the former die is a glaring injustice. A turtle, for instance, is a developmental successor to a stone. Why can the predecessor go on endlessly, while the turtle has to say goodbye at some point? Although the turtle doesn't actually have it that bad. What about a fly? Assuming the optimistic variant, it will live up to a month at the longest. So there's no need to get upset if you don't manage to swat it. The pest isn't going to last long, anyway.

What's all this dying about? Let's remember what developmental outcomes Nature expects. The best possible ones, to put it concisely. Some may find the method a bit brutal, but the threat of complete elimination is certainly a great motivator. It's really hard to imagine a zebra going to extraordinary lengths to escape a lion if the consequence of getting caught was, say, being knocked into the grass. Or listening to the triumphant roar of the lion that it was faster after all.

Chapter Eight

Some might object that I'm not presenting the issue in a fair way. A lot of animals don't like meat, and consumption takes place under far less dramatic circumstances. First of all, not really. Quite a few plants work hard to make eating them not so easy. They equip themselves with spikes, stingers, and poisonous substances (or at least with ones that fool the senses). Secondly, there are other factors besides reliability that an author needs to take into consideration. A gorilla chewing shoots for hours on end is hardly an exciting picture. Without a good dose of drama, the reader is going to be bored pretty soon. There is a reason why nature documentaries show a lot of sinking fangs and tearing apart or ripping out of guts (everything still alive) rather than just grazing or nibbling on leaves. Reliability and fairness? Let's just say, the rent and bills aren't going to pay themselves, are they, dear journalists?

Bloodshed aside, biological evolution has been a very efficient and smooth process. Each participant has had their own genetic file. All changes resulting from interactions with the environment and efforts of every kind have been noted. Through procreation, the files were passed on to successors, who enriched them with their own achievements.

Suppose that our persistent anteater elongated its snout by two-tenths of a millimeter throughout its lifetime. Its last offspring would be born with that much longer one. I mean, it would be born with a shorter one because it was small, but then it would catch up. If it tried to get to ants and termites as hard as its father did, its last offspring's snout would be 400 microns longer than its grandpa's. How many millimeters is 400 microns? If you read attentively (and can count a little), you already know. If you don't, just return to the beginning of this paragraph. You are allowed to use a calculator, but you aren't going to get the same developmental effect.

In the meantime, I have a riddle for the attentive math lovers. How many years must it have taken for an anteater snout to grow by five centimeters? Keeping in mind that the previous riddle was a total failure, I'll try to give you more data this time around. Let's assume that each individual was equally persistent at trying to get food. A wild anteater—the one from the zoo, demoralized by humans, isn't suitable for any statistics—lives an average of fifteen years. It is procreating for ten years, and it has been doing it for a very long time (the latter piece of information is completely irrelevant). I wasn't planning on giving you a second chance, dear reader. I hope you've learned your lesson and you are not going to waste this one. When you are done counting, write your result here: _____.

The individual efforts of each animal mainly rewarded their offspring. Our anteater couldn't hope to relax in its old age and benefit from its hard work. There was no old age. As it retired from procreating, it grew weaker and became easy prey for the hard-working predators out there. Its successors succumbed to the same fate, and that was anything but cool. Or maybe it wasn't? How the hell should I know? Did the anteater come to me and complain about its fate? Maybe it was happy as a clam with the whole situation and didn't have the slightest desire to change anything at all.

"If so, it clearly didn't realize the extent of its plight," some enlightened activist preoccupied with fixing the fates of others would say. "For its sake, we should make it aware of the situation, and then help it get out of its misery and backwardness." And what if it insisted that it was doing well? "Then, for its greater good, it would be necessary to help it by force." Sailing explorers may also have been guided by the same noble motives. They tried to help various more or less backward individuals, and the latter, fallen into that backwardness, couldn't understand the good that was being done for them. And so, dear reader, in my literary and moral zeal I have somehow managed to jump from the anteater to colonialism. I'm not quite sure what the point was. Anyway, I only spent six sentences on it. I'm getting better and better with words.

The anteater's efforts and that of its predecessors and successors influenced the development of the species. Or underdevelopment and downfall if they were lazy. The same goes for its cousin, the sloth, and quite frankly, I have no idea why they call it that. It still exists, doesn't it? All organisms, whether standing or moving (even very slowly), were subject to the same iron rules. Those that went in the wrong direction, or were a bit too lazy, were wiped out. The rest made an active effort to develop. Every creature, even those that followed the right path and toiled like an ox, had only as much time at their disposal as they were fit and efficient enough. Then they too were eliminated. Relentless optimization regardless of the cost.

That's how Nature works. Brr, it gives me the creeps; I just can't quite place the feeling, whether it's fear or admiration. If prehuman beings had the capacity for abstract thinking, they might have thought for a moment and asked themselves what the point of it all is. And then they might have come to the sad conclusion that, from their perspective, there is none. All this development is just some crazy perpetuum mobile, bloody and brutal, regenerating for its own sake, over and over, with no end in sight… "Objection, Your Honor! They could have thought about that, but for some reason Nature didn't equip them with that ability. And the end was in sight—the human."

Part IV

HUMAN

Chapter Nine

Imagine, dear reader, taking a trip to an amusement park. It's teeming with rides, slides, and rollercoasters. So far you've only been on your way; now you're getting inside. If you are a faint-hearted person, check the supply of calming herbs and put the kettle on. They take a long time to infuse properly? No worries. We aren't going to jump straight on the biggest dipper.

If you want to say a prayer just in case, go ahead: "The driving force behind all processes occurring in Nature is the urge to evolve. It is an ongoing process of interactions and verifications. It creates new structures, improves existing ones, or destroys them if the checks fail. This scheme guarantees the best possible outcome and further optimal development. It concerns every form of matter, as well as humans."

Amen. Who or what is a human? I ask this question in two variants because some believe that a human is some sort of machine or device. A clockwork teddy bear, if you will, only slightly more complex. The proponents of this concept argue that we are nothing but a bunch of atoms. All the processes that take place in and around us are their work alone. They claim that there is no significant distinction between a saddle, a horse, and a rider. The only difference lies in the complexity of the operations each machine needs to handle.

At a glance, this argument seems to hold water—maybe except for the fact that it doesn't make any sense. Not the argument itself, which is pretty neat. What lacks sense is the reality that surrounds us, and our presence in it. To be honest, if we are machines, what's the point of all this? What's the goal here? Making ourselves comfortable on Earth? You've got to be kidding me. We don't really fit in here. Without humans in the picture, one could maybe consider this alternative. Our presence completely ruins it. Other locations? You've got to be kidding me again. If it were possible to live there, something (and then someone) would have taken advantage of that option a long time ago.

"There is no goal," an educated thinker would say. "It just kind of stirs around and with time it's going to stop. Everything about this stirring is random. Earth is a fluke and life just happened. Humans evolved because some branch broke one day, and a monkey fell out of a tree, got a concussion, and its brain suddenly started developing at an astounding pace. Had it been sitting on a different branch or jumped off the breaking one just a moment earlier, the *Homo sapiens* would never have come to be. That is just the way it is."

There is still a more in-depth analysis possible by some lost-in-thought theorist of something. He might conclude that the goal is to find out what the goal is. You know what? Why not! If you can eagerly contemplate whether it's better for something to be there or not to be there—without first specifying what that something is—you can also try to explore the goal of the goal. You just have to get some money somewhere.

I don't buy the theory of random stirring. There's not an ounce of logic to it. When you observe Nature, you can only marvel at how everything is perfectly tuned and works just as perfectly. Like a Swiss watch, if you will. (By the way, its goal is not perfection, but time measuring.) Some might say: "All right. And what about a human? If Nature is so perfect, how did this dud come about?" This is a wrong take. *Homo sapiens* has just been born and is still in its infancy. You cannot accuse toddlers of a lack of good manners when they scream out loud for food. They just haven't learned to talk yet.

Before they do, I suggest a brief repetition of the controversial forces of Nature. Let's quickly rewind the last few billion years (and you thought the speed of light was fast). Actually, this billions thing is more like reading tea leaves, so let's go back an awful lot of years. Matter came to life because it had advanced to the point where it could respond to the stimulation of a new powerful force. *New* doesn't mean that somebody had just set it in motion or restarted it after a long period without use. It is a constantly active part of Nature, like all other forces. It remains available to those who are able to use it. That's the only reasonable explanation, unless we want to resort to random stirring. You cannot deny the existence of something just because you are not able to measure or grasp it with your mind.

Let's imagine that Newton was never born. We also suspect that the Earth is a sphere. We're watching a suicide attempt by means of a jump from the tenth floor. Without checking whether the try was successful—I bet yes—a different question emerges. Why did the individual frustrated with his life move down so sharply? Why not up? Although, if the unfortunate event had occurred at the bottom of the sphere, he would have moved upward. On the other hand, with a sphere in space, the bottom and the top are somewhat fluid concepts. It's all a matter of perspective. And there is still another issue with... well, you already know, dear reader, why I sometimes tend to simplify things. Let's combine the direction of the fall and the fact that we can observe it with a bit of logical thought. The only reasonable conclusion is that the suicide and the observer are drawn toward the Earth. You don't exactly need a degree in physics and mathematics or any sophisticated measuring instruments to determine this. "Imagination is more important than knowledge," as my ancestor would say.

The existence of a life force has serious implications. Nature is never wrong or mistaken. It wouldn't create it for nothing or just in case. It was certain to come in handy sooner or later, just like all the others already in use. The formation of Earth and the emergence of life on it was therefore not a matter of chance, but of time. The appearance of a human (as long as it wasn't a consequence of this broken branch) signifies another force, much more powerful than all the others. It was clear that it would come in handy one day—with no apparent need, no one would install it either. Which means that humans are the inevitable result of the evolution of living beings—from bacteria to the first humanoid.

I don't like the word "humanoid." The "last monkey" is an inaccurate term and sounds even worse. But I have to name him somehow. Let it be Adam. There might be some issues with Eve. I don't need her for anything at this point and would happily skip her. On the other hand, I cannot really afford to lose most of my readers just like that. The statistics on which gender is more likely to read books are clear. So let me cleverly suggest that Eve was the first human. Unfortunately, I don't have the rights to use her profile.

Chapter Ten

Let's compare an erratic boulder to a chimpanzee. And now a chimpanzee to a human. Even though some people see the chimpanzee as a sort of cousin, the latter pairing has much less in common. I refer to potential because in practice it might vary. Humans drew away from chimpanzees at lightning speed. However, we would never have accomplished that if we didn't have a decent power assistance. I can see a similar situation when I ride my bike and I'm pushing hard to go up a hill when I am mercilessly overtaken by often much older people, both males and females. Worse still, they hardly slow down when climbing the hill. They don't seem to get particularly tired either. In the meantime, fighting hard and losing my breath, I am left behind, thinking depressively about my fitness, or rather lack thereof. Needlessly though—all it would take to see the reason was a closer look. Some bicycles are equipped with batteries nowadays.

Looking only at the elementary building elements, a boulder, a chimpanzee, and a human hardly differ. Maybe the bricks are shaped and fired differently—the clay is still the same. Adding biology, the distance increases drastically. But only to the boulder. A chimpanzee and a human are still very similar. The difference relates mainly to the brain, the organ that does (or could) benefit humans the most. I'm talking about physiological similarity. From an aesthetic point of view, there is a legitimate distinction in favor of humans. I wonder what the chimp would say about this.

The biological comparison results, say, in a draw. All right, with a slight tilt toward us. Looking beyond matter and biology, our primate cousin doesn't really exist. It is gone, melted, vaporized. I could go the easy way and mention Bach, Rembrandt or the architecture of Florence, but I am not going to torment the poor animal. It's easy to kick the weaker link, especially when it is already down, counted slowly to ten. And it wasn't the chimp's fault—it never stood a chance. This is simply not its weight class. Or rather, insufficient access level. The proper one offers really good opportunities. Over four billion or rather an awful lot of years, living beings have managed to go from bacteria to monkey. We needed two and a half thousand times shorter than that to land on the Moon. (Another question is—what for?)

Reducing humans to just a biological follow-up to the primates, we haven't undergone some outstanding metamorphosis over these few million years. We straightened up a bit, pulled lower jaws back, and pushed foreheads out. Plus a few minor cosmetic corrections. As a result, some wise guys enrolled us in the family of Great Apes, or hominids if you like it more sophisticated. Along with bonobos, chimpanzees, gorillas, and orangutans. We don't get to choose our families, but let me tell you, we could have ended up worse off than that. "Hominids exhibit great intelligence, a tendency to adopt an upright and bipedal posture, as well as the ability to make and use tools."

Well, I wouldn't overstate human inclination toward *uprighting*. We definitely prefer a sedentary lifestyle. And I wasn't aware that our primate cousins were making tools. Too bad, I would love to see some product lines they offer. As for intelligence, I cannot help but fully agree, especially when it comes to some *Homo sapiens* representatives who quite seriously call for human rights to be granted to other members of the family. I think it shouldn't be left at that. I would suggest giving them a certain number of seats in our parliaments. By the way, it's not a novel idea. In his time, the

Roman Emperor Caligula apparently appointed his horse as a senator.

Some countries have already taken the first step in that noble pursuit. They exclude our great-ape cousins from medical experiments—which I strongly support, if for totally different reasons. On the other hand, banning only the closest of family members reeks of obvious nepotism. What about the gibbons? They are short, that's true, but is it their fault? And what about our more distant cousins in the tree of evolution? Why do their different preferences, such as having a tail and a more horizontal posture, lead to them being brought under the knife, or should I say, the syringe? If you believe that a rat is more different from a gorilla than the latter from you... well, the human mind is truly a curious thing.

No animal should be the subject of medical experiments. What some butchers in white coats—oh, sorry, researchers—are doing to them is simply shameful. And just so we're clear: I am not some kind of fanatic, or even a passionate advocate for them (I mean the animals, not the butchers). I simply believe that it's wrong to mistreat the weak, even if you are capable of doing so. No idea, no matter how noble, can justify it. (By the way, the idea isn't noble, it is simply crappy.) This is, among other things, what humanity is all about.

How did the first human show up? According to a version that was dominant until recently, this was done by some magic touch (or breath). If we remove the wizard, I might even be tempted to entertain the idea. At some point Adam's brain received the first impulse —be it a magical one. Our protagonist probably didn't realize the seriousness of the situation and simply ignored the signal, like many that followed. That doesn't change the fact that he began to exist as a human being. The same thing happened with Eve (I can now write about her because I just got the license) and their colleagues. Some missed the opportunity for good. Others—for a long time and in blissful ignorance—received more signals, not really knowing what to do with them. Who knows, maybe in some cases, they are ignorant to this very day.

It kind of reminds me of our biological dawn. The first impulse is the equivalent of the victorious marathon of the sperm to fuse with the egg. Some embryos that don't withstand the initial or subsequent checks are naturally lost. Or less naturally if there is another human at work (or even not lost, to remain unbiased). The others, not knowing who they are or would be, slowly develop in the solitude of their mothers, gradually acquiring a human form. Then they are born. Taking an appropriate time perspective for the nine months of pregnancy—let's say, hundreds of thousands, maybe even a million or more years (it doesn't really matter)—this is roughly what it looked like for the first humans, before they began to realize that something significant made them stand out from the other creatures. Even those with very similar DNA.

This doesn't change the fact that the difference is anything but spectacular at the moment. I can even understand why these learned clerks registered us and other primates at one address. In all fairness, we land on the top floor—remember the hotel I mentioned earlier? At this point I can already hear the slightly confused readers. "Wait a second! What about the flight to the Moon? And these two and a half thousand times—where have they gone? What about Bach and Rembrandt?"

First of all, don't get too excited or take a sip of your herbal infusion. (I hope you followed my advice and brewed one.) Secondly, there is no contradiction here. Let's not confuse potential with reality. The trip into space is just a clever marketing ploy. The scene is easy to visualize and gets your imagination going. Two and a half thousand times also sounds fairly impressive, doesn't it? Besides, the same rocket flight can be used to support a completely opposite argument that we are in fact regressing as a species. We could illustrate it with clouds of smoke billowing from under the rocket, which results in exceeding the level of something by 7,412 times. Next we could show a piece of a broken-off glacier, and for the grand finale, snappy coverage from a heavily flooded city.

And the thing with the great artists is just another thought trap, which I set up deliberately. Without being vigilant enough, you fall right into it. Let's add up all the relevant creators, such as composers, painters, writers, engineers, and whoever else might be.

Now we compare that number with the total of the *Homo sapiens* representatives. There aren't many of the former. Very few, in fact. Maybe not on one hand, but it won't be much. And their accomplishments, with all due respect, are not an indicator of the quality of the rest. These people had a knack for something, decided it was worth the effort, and climbed to great heights. We should be thankful that they were so eager. There's no further need to speculate about the incredible potential of human beings. Exploiting this potential or letting it go to waste is our choice. More precisely, that of every single one of us.

Chapter Eleven

To enjoy free choice, you had to clear the terrain first, starting with the removal of the major road hog—the threat that something bigger or stronger or both would eat you. That is why other living beings have only had the illusion of choice. Little did they know that there was a remedy for this. As I said before—not the proper access level. Humans, even if it took a while, managed to fix the issue. Actually, I don't think an irresistible longing for freedom was the driving force here. I rather suspect a far more mundane desire to eliminate some discomfort when you are consumed.

But if I'm wrong, I can already picture a guy standing at a crossroads and contemplating: "Damn, it's so irritating that I have no choice. I have to go left but I would prefer to go right. The road might be bumpier, but I would arrive much quicker—if it weren't for that goddamn smilodon just around the bend. There's no way it won't turn me into its dinner. Come on, I need to do something about it. I'm not going to let some four-legged chump block my way just because it is stronger." Then, I see him think for a while, dig a trench nearby, cover it with branches, place on them something freshly hunted and still a bit alive, and finally stimulate the aforementioned big tiger to be interested in this place.

This is certainly a somewhat simplified version of how humans got rid of the large predators threatening their lives. The fact is, they did it. The owner of a sharp mind might say that this story is inconsistent. Our protagonist had a choice—even though he thought he didn't. He could have decided not to dig the hole. To which I say, he would then have to go left. So, he would have no choice. On the other hand, he could always go home, which means he had a choice after all. Besides, he could have stayed at home and never left in the first place. And that's how we are again searching for the goal of the goal. This often happens when you make up hypothetical yet very unlikely situations.

One day, fighting against the imperfection in the use of foreign language, I was following a lecture at a renowned university, something about moral dilemmas. The professor asked the students to decide whether, being a signalman, they would let a speeding trolley run on a track with five people standing at the end of it, which would inevitably cause their death. (Why would they wait for the trolley to hit them?) Alternatively, the students could divert it to another track where it would kill only one person... Something along these lines. I have no idea whether a career as a lower-level railway employee was a seriously considered option for graduates of this prestigious school. I'm not trying to judge anybody, but that seems unlikely. Just like accidentally finding themselves near a railroad switch with a trolley setting off on its own (the signalman was on his lunch break).

Another challenge for humans was to capture fire. It enflamed uncontrollably, which was a shame, as it seemed to have a multifunctional use—to warm up food and oneself, scare away wild animals, or light up the evening dusk. There were two options available: lying down and waiting for the next accurate lightning strike, or rubbing, which was an uncomfortable activity but had a much greater developmental potential. When it came to speech, people could also have followed the chimps and left it down to a few grunts. Or get themselves together and expand the repertoire. The second tendency prevailed, but I wonder if humans didn't go overboard in this pursuit—we ended up with thousands of different languages.

By far the greatest masterpiece of early humankind was the reform of the food supply system. For animals, finding something to eat took up most of their time, ranking far ahead of avoiding getting eaten and procreating (even with accompanying activities). At first, humans didn't do too well in that department. They wandered for hours in search of some edible plants, or chased game in the meadows and forests. It was not only tiresome but dangerous. In all the collecting or hunting eagerness, you could easily overlook a large predator that hadn't ended up in a hole yet. And your own success was anything but certain.

Something had to be done, and people came up with a really evil plan. It was about first becoming friends with the potential victims and then, once they were lulled by the deceptive feeling of close ties, killing and eating them. In terms of logistics, the entire operation needed to be completed as close to home as possible. This reduced the risk of victims falling into the wrong hands (or paws). As for plants, the issue wasn't too complicated. Mesmerized by the fertile soil and weeded competition, they were eager to grow. With animals, it required far more patience and talent. Happy to eat the food left for them, they preferred to spend the night at home. It took some time, but eventually convenience and laziness prevailed, with more and more animals choosing the all-inclusive package. After people expanded the offering to include procreation without fighting (even as much as a scuffle), the new generations had no idea that there was any other place to live.

It reminds me of a scene from a film about hamburgers, featuring some noble-hearted activists breaking down the fence and persuading the soon-to-be beef to leave the bondage and march toward freedom. To their disappointment, the offer wasn't met with any particular enthusiasm. (Thank God, we're speaking about animals, and it was just a film.) On the other hand, I can understand them a little. Freedom advocates often forget to mention the other side of the coin. A guard dog lives behind the fence with a chain around its neck. But it enjoys a well-padded kennel and a bowl of warm food, guaranteed every day. If it looks well enough, they might even let it mate from time to time. A stray mongrel will sometimes find a fatty bone in the garbage, sometimes a rotten potato. The rain will drench its fur, and the sun will dry it. As for dating, there is not only more choice but also fierce competition. To each his own.

Chapter Twelve

Various activities of living organisms stimulated their bodies to change. The giraffe's neck elongated, the eagle's beak sharpened, the snake's tongue forked, and the crocodile increased the strength of its jaw. They practiced something akin to bodybuilding. It wasn't a conscious effort to work on their figures or teeth; it happened rather by accident—mostly while foraging for food. We can only envy our predecessors. It would be much more enjoyable to sculpt our physiques by buying potatoes, eggs, or a pound of pork neck (with or without the bone) rather than by sweating our guts out at the gym, doing cardio or CrossFit, or dragging weights. Not to mention riding a bike for dozens of miles without moving as much as an inch.

Instead of modifying their bodies, humans went the other way. Or rather, they took a shortcut. People didn't want to wait indefinitely for this or that to sharpen, elongate, or grow stronger and decided to use whatever was readily available: sticks, stones, or pieces of metal. With a little processing, they managed to bang together pretty nifty devices, much more effective than the sharpest teeth or the most ripped of muscles. Then they dominated the entire plant and animal world in record time. Humans not only overpowered their equals and smaller creatures but also much bigger ones. The

Chapter Twelve

elephant, for example, was used as a means of transportation or a construction machine. I'm quite certain that if people lived in the dinosaur era, they would have found some work for them, too.

Okay, now you've gone a bit overboard, dear author. If dinosaurs had lived on, humankind would have never come to exist, so there would be no one to find any work for them. On the other hand, since the appearance of humans was all but inevitable, the dinosaurs needed to go. Without diving further into mental gymnastics, this is the only time I would be willing to accept the intervention of a higher power in the evolutionary processes on Earth. It watched with growing impatience as the existence of the oversized extended mercilessly, preventing the events from unfolding as intended. And then, it slightly manipulated the trajectory of a certain meteorite.

After taming the animals, humans carried out a clothing revolution. It was inspired by a desire to travel and, again, a lack of patience. The northern regions turned out to be slightly cooler, and people didn't want to wait for their own insulation to grow. They instead borrowed skins and furs from the locals—weasels, foxes, and others alike. To avoid annoying bureaucracy—who borrowed from whom and for how long—debtors were in the habit of getting rid of the creditors. At first, everyone had only one someone else's fur. Later, a purely utilitarian approach quickly gave way and fashion emerged, and an increasingly rich assortment of garments became available. Gradually, furs were replaced by plant-based products. Having multiple outfits and being able to change quickly turned out to be very appealing to people—in particular, to their female section, as well as wardrobe manufacturers.

Since we didn't focus on beaks and claws, what did humans develop? It was obviously the brain. Compared to the chimpanzee, ours is three times as big. "So what?" I hear someone ask rationally. "An elephant's brain is five times bigger than ours, and I wouldn't call it a mental giant." "Because the elephant is a large animal," explains someone else. "Proportions matter." "Miss!" a zoologist who happened to pass by will interject. "A mouse has a similar brain-to-body ratio as a human." I might also add that small birds boast an even better ratio than we do. Just like ants. Where is their intelligence and wit?

"Then why do humans behave differently from animals?" I hear you ask this time. Because we're not animals. Just like a turtle isn't a stone, even though sometimes it can be difficult to tell them apart, especially if the former hides in the shell. (Well, unless you kick the stone and the turtle turns out to have bad nerves.) By the way, it's truly fascinating how it came up with this armor of sorts. Underneath it is nigh *unbiteable*. If it came up with extra anchoring hooks, it would be rendered practically unbeatable.

"Wait a second!" I can hear some indignant researcher yelling from the distance. "What is this nonsense!? Are we back in the Dark Ages again!? Humans are very much animals. Just somewhat better-developed!" Then he will list plenty of astonishing similarities that his colleagues have worked tirelessly to discover. Dear reader, in your ignorance, you probably had no idea that when a mouse feels pain, it pulls faces just like we do. Fortunately (or not—it's all a matter of perspective), someone very smart found this out. Now, when they are inflicting pain, it's very easy to figure out if the mouse is suffering, or if it just fakes it really well. Or take the cows. It was observed that they moo with different accents, depending on the region they live in. Just like locals from Boston or Texas, you can instantly hear where they come from. Of course, the list would be incomplete without our good friend the chimpanzee. It arranges stones, somewhat disorderly and with no practical use—irrefutable proof of religious practices. Unfortunately, it wasn't specified whether it worships only on Sundays. It is also unclear whom the pious monkey adores. Perhaps the researcher conducting the experiment?

I just reread the previous paragraph. Then I looked in the mirror, honestly fearing to see a mule—an exceptionally stubborn one at that. If such overwhelming evidence isn't enough to convince me... I think I'm more inclined (especially when I remember the praying chimpanzee) to believe that animals are humans—just slightly underdeveloped. You see, now this mule thing seems to be more fitting. In fact, it's all about the pace. The changes taking place in Nature are usually very slow. This has been the case for an awful lot of years, bar none. Why should that change for one particular animal? Did Nature, encouraged by the spectacular success of exterminating the dinosaurs, decide to make another exception?

Unless we are nothing but a deviation—some kind of tumor on a healthy, natural tissue. A nasty growth that expands abnormally fast. I don't dare think what the humans-are-animals proponents are going to say about it. They all are dignified researchers, equipped with keen, inquisitive minds. How do they admit that they're just blackheads or glistening boils? Their counterparts who specialize in medicine would probably suggest squeezing or piercing them, while the more malicious specimens should be poisoned, irradiated, or treated with a scalpel. If the anomaly proves true, Nature will take care of it—it's only a matter of time. But I have my doubts. I listened to Mozart's Requiem the other day. I'm not sure if such music could be written by an evolutionary deviant.

While I doggedly insist that humans are not animals, some virtuosi of advanced thought go a step further, or rather backward in this case. They suggest that people are machines—and all other living things as well. This proposal doesn't make much sense, but I will give it some thought just to stretch my mind a bit. A machine is usually a device constructed by someone to carry out a given task more quickly and conveniently. Take lifting a load, for example. In the case of a human, the machine made itself, and it happened by accident. There's no other logical conclusion to be derived here. Well, unless it was made by someone, but this belief is vehemently rejected by the adherents of the machine theory.

In the past, humans have had flashes of thought that they are machines. But it took until recently for a group of enlightened people to fully realize it, and what implications arise from that realization. This is a turning point in the history of humanity, or *humachinity*, if you will. There is no need to leave the course of events to chance anymore, or to be at the mercy of some undefined fate—or lack thereof. Finally we can take matters into our own hands, or into controlled upper limbs, to be more precise. There's a lot of work to be done. Even a cursory observation shows that we are just lemons. Our brain is a snail compared to a fast computer. Our teeth fall out, hearing dulls, and eyes become blurry. Not to mention the cancers we produce ourselves running some suicidal amok. As if that wasn't enough, after a while we are unusable at all, ending up in a cemetery or crematorium, depending on the method of disposal.

All this will need to be fixed. Fortunately, we're very smart now, so we'll make it. Artificial intelligence will replace our outdated one. We will grow new kidneys, pancreases, and livers in labs. We will manipulate the genes so that every fiftieth birthday will automatically be replaced by the thirtieth. We also need to take care of our cousins, the *animachines*, starting from the tiny ones that attack us insidiously and unexpectedly, taking advantage of their miserable stature and nasty character. We must track them down, resocialize them if possible, and if not, exterminate them by means of disinfection. Well, this may sound brutal, but like any revolution, this one also requires victims.

Of course, we can't be selfish and forget our non-living brothers and sisters who have fallen behind in the process. We will implant artificial intelligence in them as well. Additionally, we will equip them with prosthetics for walking and flying. And then... I can already see shovels digging pits on their own, drills perforating holes in walls all by themselves, and a coach that moves without a horse and a coachman. The horse, also artificially intelligent, would run riding lessons at this time. Unfortunately, this alluring vision is unlikely to come to fruition. Their trendsetting *humachines* have a serious error in construction. They are missing some of their buttons.

Chapter Thirteen

How many kinds of creatures are there on Earth? The most accurate estimate is an awful lot. Giving any numbers seems akin to reading tea leaves and is of similar value. I've already cited eight million, then a billion. "Will ya give me more?" Right, we're not in an auction house. Another source (the figures are just as reliable and trustworthy) presented an even greater spread—there is, was, or maybe both, between two million and ten to the power of twelve species. Which is 10,000,000,000,000; in words, ten trillion. In other words, an incredible awful lot. The same source states that some 99 percent of organisms that have lived on Earth are already extinct. Which doesn't surprise me at all, considering how Nature works and the meticulous quality control in place. At the same time it thoroughly discredits those who accuse *Homo sapiens* of being the main perpetrator of this extinction. How was the 99 percent calculated? By virtue of their long education, scholars tend to be very comfortable with numbers. A certain level of bravado isn't missing in this group either.

In fact, it's all because of computers. Since the advent of machines that could perform quick calculations, people have eagerly filled their innards with various data of more or less questionable quality. They then press the important key and wait for the result.

When you study something, you need a result, preferably an impressive one. Once you leave a good impression, better yet a breathtaking one, it will be easier to get money to continue the research. Large numbers make the best impression. So do the very small ones. Ideally, written to the power, positive or negative. You can also go for those with lots of zeros, the ones people don't know the names of. When they see them, they may feel silly for not knowing. As a result, they tend to respect individuals who mingle with quadrillions, not to mention quinvigintillions.

Since there are plenty of species that don't always get along well with each other, and even go as far as to cause each other grief and trouble, they have no other choice but to constantly improve—to grow taller, or to eat the others. Otherwise, their opponents will grow taller, or eat them. These improvements took a long time to come about, but there was finally a species that had improved enough to receive the first impulse. It was the human, and another step of the strategic objective has been concluded. Just like before, out of the multitude of celestial bodies in the universe, it was Earth where life emerged.

People inherited their predilection for achieving superiority over others from plant and animal ancestors. In the case of flora and fauna, this conduct was totally reasonable. It was an existential question: either you or me. There was no other option. It's hard to imagine nettles and thistles negotiating which side of the ditch they will occupy. Or a zebra trying to convince a lion that plants are as nutritious as meat—citing itself or the even bigger elephant as an example. People don't need to dominate others, but it's difficult to get rid of bad habits right away. We don't need to prevail because we develop something different than other living beings.

"Brain!" I hear someone repeating the claim. "Our brain develops. It's not about size or proportion, it's about content. Since we have a more developed brain, we can think abstractly and discover things." But why does our brain evolve? The anteater's snout got longer and longer because its owner insisted that the tastier insects were found deeper. It didn't sit in front of the anthill and dream about eating them. It just went at them. Our brain also evolved as a result of some effort. Not just because it decided that growing and developing was a fun thing to do. But what was that effort? And where did the opportunity to make it come from?

Biologically, we have carried on the evolution of living beings on Earth. I dare say we are the desired outcome. And then, out of nowhere, we began to develop radically differently than other organisms. This must mean that we had access to something more. You don't need to graduate from a top college or get a bunch of weird abbreviations in front of your name to figure it out. Well, unless Adam accidentally flexed his cortex at some point. Then he thought of something strange. As a result, a new connection was made in his brain, which was duly noted in his genome. A bit bored, he visited Eve. They had fun and, sometime later, a child who already had this genetic change. (There is another version of this story. It was Eve who was a bit bored, so she visited Adam. You can choose whichever version you prefer.) That would mean, however, that the chimpanzee was left behind because it didn't want to flex its cortex and left it for later. No chance; it doesn't work like that. If that were the case, the good old chimp would've been gone a long time ago.

No matter how hard our primate cousin flexed its brain and how much effort it put into the process, it didn't stand a chance. Adam had access, and the ape didn't. Of course, our forefather could easily have squandered it. He received the first impulse, then the next ones. He might have ignored or overlooked them out of lack of concentration or laziness. And then he would never have become Adam. We would never have heard about him. Fortunately, that didn't happen. His choice wasn't really conscious, rather more intuitive than well thought out. Nevertheless, he made it. As a reward, he was given the honor of being the first man on Earth. This puts him in line with other distinguished personalities of this kind, such as the first man in space or on the Moon.

Chapter Fourteen

What are these impulses, and what access am I talking about? I'm not going to offer you a precise description because it's not pleasant heading for a sure failure. Of course, I could go for a proven approach and try some fairy tale. It just has to fit the taste of the masses. To enhance the effect, I could also activate some experts in the field. But I don't plan to travel to Easy Way or Astray on my thought journey. So I'm going to make an effort and go with a metaphor. It refers to existing concepts and things. Readers from the future should consult the archives or use their imagination if the archives are not accessible for some reason.

Most computer users probably know what the cloud is. I'm not referring to the stratus, cumulus or, God forbid, to the cumulonimbus, which can dump an amazing amount of water on everything. I'm talking about the internet cloud, where you can store your digital treasures free of charge or (if many treasures) for a small fee. This cloud isn't floating around in the sky. It is located in a box somewhere. Your computer, equipped with a network card, can access it via the internet. Unless of course the modem dies or the breaker suddenly pops.

The box is also something like a computer—just bigger and more powerful. The digital comrades call it a server. To make it even larger and more powerful, the servers are combined into clusters, which are stuffed into ICD cabinets, which are located in special rooms, so-called server rooms. (Not to be confused with special rooms in some restaurants, where servers can chill out during a long shift or cool down after an altercation with a particularly difficult patron.)

Now, dear reader, try to fire up your imagination. Did it work? Very well! Keep it running at full speed! Don't worry if you get tired and need to rest a bit. You can always read this paragraph again. Imagine a server room that isn't a collection of cabinets or boxes but some intangible reality surrounding us from everywhere. Or not surrounding and not from everywhere; it doesn't matter. All we need is a continuous connection to it. Our brain is, let's say, a kind of computer. The difference is that it is alive and therefore able to develop on its own. The aforementioned network card is an integral part of it. Initially, it has a tiny capacity, which can grow over time if the user desires. This is what makes us different from animals—we have the card (or something else, it doesn't matter what it is), they don't. I presume everything is clear thus far. If not, don't despair over a temporary failure, just try again.

In this mysterious, intangible reality, everyone has their own cloud, big or small—it depends on the effort put in to date. In the cloud, our individual nonmaterial assets are stored. We can use them anytime (or not, it's up to you). The more we exert ourselves, the more profits, or losses, we accumulate. This causes our brains to develop, which gives us better access, leading to the ability to accumulate more values... and so on. That is the optimistic variant. Sometimes we may be too lazy to do it. I'm not even sure which trend is more popular.

"Why do we need an alternate reality?" I hear some curious reader ask. "And what are these values we are supposed to collect there?" And then, God forbid, he might even get belligerent. "What is with all that crap about the intangible stuff? Everything takes place in our brains. There are no connections to anything because this anything doesn't exist!" Well, any conclusions we can draw from this statement are not particularly optimistic. I've mentioned this before. If we are merely hyperdeveloped representatives of fauna, our presence on Earth looks like some kind of a quirk, which isn't going to last too long.

What other animal, poorly or even moderately developed, would come up with the idea of systematic killing of its conspecifics? Or raping them? Or classifying some of them as slaves devoid of all rights, alternatively as subhuman or rather subanimal? What about abuse and torture in its multitude of forms? Just to mention a few: crushing limbs, chest, or head with fancy metal or wood devices; upside-down hanging and slowly slicing with a saw; skinning alive; or cooking in tar or other well-suited liquid. This is but a portion of the human ingenuity in inflicting suffering and pain on others. The specialized museum facilities showcase a much broader spectrum of our creativity in this field. Besides, such practices weren't just an intimate form of obtaining necessary evidence or punishing the guilty in the depths of prison dungeons. Public abuse of people of both sexes enjoyed substantial popularity. It was a welcomed attraction for the elites and crowd alike, as people were thirsty for any form of entertainment.

In later times, as general awareness and technology evolved hand in hand, the human race has discovered a predilection for killing one another more indiscriminately—by dropping exploding stuff or spreading paralyzing and poisonous agents. Thankfully, this dark past is long behind us. Now we are wiser and well aware that it's not nice to behave like that. Of course, intensive work on the next generation of lethal devices is in full swing, but that's all just a smokescreen. In reality, we are fighting for peace. Which means a lack of fighting. (It somehow reminds me of searching for the goal of the goal.) Perhaps it would be prudent to cease making devices that kill other people. The problem is, if we cease, are the others going to follow suit? Because if they don't, we'll have to cease the ceasing, and all the cessation will cease to make any sense. And something tells us that they aren't going to cease.

Unfortunately, we don't trust each other. Do you know, dear reader, how many active attorneys there are in the world? Over a million in the United States alone. Let's say there are five million attorneys in total—a very conservative estimate. Suppose each of them works only 300 days a year, eight hours a day. This adds up to twelve billion attorney man-hours per year, all because someone tries to fool, scam, or cheat someone else. Now, let's assign all these hours to only one person who works 24/7 (no Sundays, vacations, or public holidays). The total time is 1,370,000 years—roughly as much as some people estimate the entire existence of the human race on Earth. The latter statistic actually doesn't make much sense. I only brought it up because the numbers are really impressive. Nobody's going to give it a serious thought anyway.

If you're the kind of person who prefers an empirical experience over statistics or impressive figures—and by that I mean looking out the window to find out whether it's raining rather than checking the current weather conditions on an electronic device connected to the internet—you can test your own trust in other people using a simple example like the one below. (I've broken my own sentence-length record, now it's sixty-five words!)

Imagine now, dear reader, that you own a chest full of gold bars. You don't share this information with your neighbors... or your local tax authority, for that matter. As a small operational deception, you decide to part with your treasure (only briefly, of course). You're considering depositing it with another person. For this little favor, the custodian is going to receive ten percent of the contents of the chest. In order to not leave any traces, the deal remains verbal. I might add that you're not a well-known local goodfella, infamous for arranging meetings with Davy Jones in a nearby lake for your enemies dressed in concrete shoes for this occasion. Would you ask a random person to keep the chest for you? I believe that in most cases, you would have trouble asking your friends and relatives, even if they are really close to you.

Chapter Fifteen

Knowing that we cannot avoid death is very depressing for most people. This discomfort increases with age. You start to realize that, even in the optimistic variant of Methuselah, you have less and less time in this world. If someone postponed procreation, it may lead to confusing situations. "Honey, we'll return to this conversation when you're my age," says a 60-year-old to her 20-year-old daughter. Well, that's rather optimistic. Many use the ostrich method when dealing with their own mortality, pretending the issue doesn't exist. Their subconscious, however, won't let them forget about the inevitable descent, only intensifying deadly fear and discomfort.

"How much easier life would be if we weren't privy to the embarrassing knowledge that we will die," I've heard some people claim. Well, everything has its price. Animals don't seem to be bothered by the question of death, if I may make such a bold observation. Some researchers argue otherwise, citing examples of dolphins, elephants, or our monkey ancestors. With the image of the praying chimpanzee still fresh in my memory, I dare to treat such revelations with a great deal of suspicion.

In Nature, everything takes place according to certain rules and order. I see no exception to that, anywhere. The fact that we are aware of our mortality is the natural consequence of this order. Just like the fact that other living beings aren't aware of that fact. There must be some logic and sense in it. So instead of despairing, protesting, and eventually going numb, let's try to find that sense.

Before we start, let's consider why death has such a bad reputation among people. If you ask me, the main reason is the miserable PR. Imagine making your trademark a figure that completely lacks soft tissue. A human skeleton wearing a hooded black cloak and waving around a pretty nasty-looking agricultural device. Why a scythe when there's such a large assortment of cutting tools? Why not a sickle? After all, it's far handier and easier to carry while going from one household to another. Perhaps it was more about efficiency? Or maybe its dreadful and awe-inspiring look? All of this makes a good subject for closer examination by scholars active in the field.

The next step to improve death's image should involve promoting a more pleasant nomenclature. Let's start by retiring Grim Reaper—why so serious? Let's make the Reaper a bit more cheerful, give the Pale Horseman some colors, and turn the Angel of Death into an Angel of Respite. After all, which one, dear reader, would you rather meet at the end of your earthly journey? Much more emphasis also needs to be placed on death's reliability. How often do we complain that we can't trust anyone. We've all encountered snags and delays and had our plans fall apart because of others. Death is reliable. It never forgets, and it will never let you down—even if you would very much like it to. References? You will find new ones in the local newspaper every day.

Who said that you have to fear death anyway? Let's take the reports of those who've had the opportunity to familiarize themselves with the subject. They died, but somewhat half-heartedly, and after a while returned to the land of the living. And guess what—they didn't actually experience anything dramatic! On the contrary, they spoke about the situation in superlatives. They also asserted that the fear of death had left them for good. Well, even considering the exuberant human imagination and the inclination to make up stuff wherever we can, these stories can't be completely ignored.

After all, they are the only source of information from the other side we have.

I should probably have said "from the road to the other side," from which we are turned back when our biological packaging decides—due to medical intervention or as a result of independent resumption of life processes—to prolong our earthly existence for a time. As we enjoy the return (either our own or someone else's), we inevitably approach a key question. What does death really mean? Or, to put it more precisely, what actually dies? Even the Roman poet Quintus Horatius Flaccus, commonly known as Horace, felt that something was up. He publicly claimed that *"non omnis moriar."* I have no idea if we are both thinking of the same thing, but that doesn't bother me very much. It never hurts to bust out a famous person to prop up your argument, especially since that person lived some time ago and is no longer able to elaborate on his views.

If not everything, then which part of us says the final goodbye? Certainly, something we call our body. All the various cells, tissues, organs, and other vitals. They die, meaning that they cease to live. Except for those that use the sometimes-practiced fire treatments, they become easy prey and food for other living beings (usually the tiniest ones). Which indicates that when something is alive, its main occupation is to prevent being eaten by another something. The other main occupation, just to keep the balance, is eating another something. I mention this pattern again to remind everyone that our body is nothing more than a form of living matter. We should take care of it in moderation, for example, by keeping it in a good shape. Preferably by exercising and all the other kinds of physical effort. Less preferably by absorbing preparations or applying liniments. I definitely don't recommend cutting, sucking, or filling with the famous poison botulinum toxin, often shortened to Botox.

Our biological suit or dress—depending on who feels, or rather felt, more comfortable in what—doesn't have any great value after life ceases (except maybe as a tasty meal for the small scavengers mentioned above). Nevertheless, people are emotionally connected to the mortal remains of their loved ones. I read somewhere that these emotions are worth over $100 billion annually. That's the approximate revenue of the global funeral industry. Like all big numbers, that grand total is quite impressive. But it pales in comparison to the amount we spend on making our bodies die as late as possible, preferably never. Here we are dealing with numbers that could make the less immune dizzy or even cause premature death—and further prosperity for undertakers. We are talking about roughly $10 trillion, which is nearly twelve percent of the world's GDP. Most of that money is flushed down the drain anyway. But we feel much better knowing that we take such care of ourselves, or rather of our temporal limbs.

Chapter Sixteen

Particles of non-living matter connect with each other, though sometimes they disconnect, only to reconnect after a while, just a little differently. They continuously form new sets with varying properties and behaviors. The purpose is to create stable structures. The individual elements of these structures don't matter; everything is subordinated to the group. Collectivism at its finest, so to speak. I'd like to point out that this system only works at the level of non-living matter. Similar experiments on humans are not going to result in any particular success. Various nations have had the opportunity to test this in rather painful ways. Some, maniacally, are testing even to this day.

Living organisms have abandoned communes. They realized that not a bunch but *they* alone represent a value, and began to multiply it. Development was personalized, moving from a collective to the individual. This equally applies to the bacteria, the ant, and the jaguar, regardless of whether they work in large, not-so-large, or even one-man groups. I didn't mention bees because they have different social preferences. The vast majority of them, such as the mason, carpenter, and even sweat bees, are self-confessed singles. Only some, like our friends the honey bees, which we shamelessly rob on a regular basis, prefer larger communities.

Even when grouped, the members are mainly concerned with their own well-being. Fish swimming in a school don't care about the school but about themselves. The fact that they move together is a pure coincidence, albeit a very useful one. A wolf hunting in a pack wants to satisfy its own hunger, which is much more likely to happen in company. I wonder what is the motive of a single rat, sent out by its distrustful companions on a scouting mission to test a new food source—or rather, a culinary Russian roulette. Certainly not to get poisoned and become a martyr. Perhaps, being a weedy specimen, it takes the chance in order to get rid of the label of the group nincompoop and become the object of desire for the opposite sex at last—assuming it survives the experiment.

Regardless of whether together or separate, representatives of the same species engage in similar activities. They also evolve in similar ways. For this, they must exert themselves and overcome difficulties, which they do (if not, they are done). Development includes their biological components. They have nothing else to develop. Humans, by contrast, can perfect their nonmaterial qualities—assuming they possess any and are willing to work on them. I would strongly encourage everyone to find some will. This is a very forward-thinking activity, with a sky-high range of possibilities.

I can imagine that a few inquisitive readers would expect some clarification on the aforementioned nonmaterial qualities. I'm afraid I'll have to disappoint you. How am I supposed to know? It depends on the effort made to date and the work you've done (or refrained from doing). Let's not mix things up; this is not about some universal values. You act on your own accord. What you collect belongs to you, not others. Imagine that someone has a bank account. It could also be a trunk in the attic or a pickle jar buried in the garden. Whatever the stash, it contains a certain amount of a means of payment. As you might suppose, the owner generally doesn't run his mouth about these. He knows how many bills he possesses. Usually he also has a plan for what to do with it. If not, he can always go to a financial adviser. It is worth keeping in mind, however, that the adviser's main motive isn't going to be maximizing client assets but rather making money in the form of commission. Of course, combining the one with the other can't be ruled out.

Comparing nonmaterial assets to quite-material banknotes is hardly a wise approach. The same goes for other valuables like gold bars, Arabian champions, or fancy properties in attractive locations. As soon as we die, all of these goods disappear from our portfolio forever. Suppose that—having forgotten, out of distraction or deliberate intent, to write down the last will—they were not distributed more or less justly. The heirs would, in all likelihood, begin an acrimonious battle to inherit as many possessions as possible. This doesn't concern us anymore. At most, a tear might still well up in the gloomy eye. Our unearthly wealth, for a change, we take with us in full. No one else is going to use it. This should be a strong hint as to what one should take care of while walking this Earth. In reality, there is a preponderance of fans of more tangible assets. Well, everyone has their own preferences. Don't we have free will and the freedom of choice?

Material goods cannot be considered as permanent or of essential value. They play no role in human development. In animals, offspring benefit from their parents' efforts. The elongated muzzle or sharper claws they inherit are useful in their own development. In the case of human heirs, assets obtained from their ancestors are more likely to provoke laziness than to stimulate them to act (except for families where parents did their job *comme il faut*). And if the manager isn't prudent enough, the goods can quickly change hands.

It looks slightly better with inherited practical skills, passed down through generations from father to son. (Interestingly, no one ever talks about things passed from grandpa to father, from mother to daughter, or from uncle to nephew.) But here, too, proficiency in baking bread, rearing cattle for meat or fur, or repairing Swiss watches (these tend to never break, so let's go with maintaining instead) seems quite superficial in comparison to sharper claws. And children don't always find pleasure in carrying on parental passions.

So what do we inherit from our ancestors? Maybe intellect? Or creative potential? Let's see—to that end, we will use the example of Johann Sebastian Bach, who is regarded as one of the greatest composers in the history of music, and rightfully so. His father, Johann Ambrosius (they shared a surname) was also in the business. Except he didn't write any music; he just played it, using violin, trumpet, and something else, I think. So far, everything checks out. The son inherited the talent from his father and developed it to a greater extent. In fact, one could hardly do more than he did. The problem is that he wasn't the only descendant. His older brother, Johann Christoph Bach, was also a musician. It's very likely that he even showed the younger the ropes. But he himself didn't excel in the field, to say the least. So why did Sebastian (I use their second names because the brothers had identical first ones) climb the heights while Christoph remained in the valley?

Of course, we could assume that the younger brother simply craved success. But we don't know the details, and it's impolite—especially if you didn't know the person—to put others in a bad light. My bet would be on Sebastian's greater potential. Where did he get it? Just be patient. I wouldn't focus too hard on inheritance from the father, either. The youngsters soaked up the subject as children, that's it. By the way, Johann Sebastian had quite a lot of offspring (he was, after all, a very fertile composer). Several of his sons tried to follow in their father's creative footsteps. No dice. Did they too have problems with stimulus and passion? They were even very popular in their own day. But, as it happens in Nature, there is a time for inspection where poor-quality goods end up on the trash pile. This applies to dinosaurs and music alike.

Chapter Seventeen

Effort is conducive to growth—mostly of the person who makes this effort, though others can benefit as well. The aforementioned Johann Sebastian, a God-fearing man, wrote his fugues and cantatas for the glory of the Lord and also to please other authorities—the earthly ones—on their princely thrones, bishoprics, and castles. He most likely wasn't thinking of catering to the sophisticated tastes of future listeners. This doesn't change the fact that his music has become an inspiration to others and may even have stimulated their own development, but this was only a side effect of his effort—surely very welcome by those he inspired.

The additional beneficiaries of Bach's creative efforts are few in number, or at least I choose to believe so. In the case of his compatriot, a man named Johannes Gutenberg, there will be quite a lot of them. If you are reading the paperback version of this book, you might even be part of that group. Grappling with his fonts, Gutenberg certainly didn't think about stimulating the developmental tendencies of future readers. It's even unclear whether he evolved himself. Perhaps he was only driven by a shallow desire to multiply his earthly-material possessions? Who knows—maybe he had regressed in his development? Or even went astray? For the rest of us it doesn't matter in the slightest. There is an enormous potential in reading, especially literature, preferably fiction—as long as you want to take advantage of the opportunity.

The development of a downright enormous number of people, the likes which Gutenberg would never have dared to dream of, may have been a side effect of the effort made by another man (or woman, but this is less probable). Unfortunately, we don't know his name. He was active a long time ago, and none of his contemporaries bothered to identify him. I'm referring to the creator of the absolutely greatest invention in human history—the wheel. It happened some 6,000 years ago. Maybe 5,000, or possibly 7,643. If you're not convinced that the wheel can be a source of developmental inspiration, then get on a bike. It can be an electric one for all I care, even though a push bike is better. Then cycle to a nearby meadow, which is located a few miles away—unfortunately this is the most nearby one, but don't worry, there is also a small pond there, so you can refresh yourself if necessary. Lying next to it, just think about why the flowers growing in the meadow have different colors. It's going to take you some time, but that's okay, because the weather is playing nice. After solving the riddle, go back home.

The next day, having previously erased the result of recent deliberations from memory, repeat the action. This time you can't use the bike. Yesterday, on the way back, you caught a flat tire. Sorry, you have to walk. There'll be much less time to ponder (to deliberate next to the pond) and much smaller energy reserves. During strenuous mental effort, the human brain supposedly draws quite a lot of it. So the likelihood of obtaining similar results as the previous day will be far from certain. The same goes for the attendant increase in your potential. If you're still not convinced by this obvious example about the developmental benefit of using a wheel —or two in this case—I'd then suggest contemplating the roundness of the shape itself. It can lead to growth, too, and it's certainly relaxing.

Regardless of the number of incidental beneficiaries, the one who made the effort profits the most. Even if he took the wrong path, he might still benefit—because once astray, he might notice this and change direction in another bout of effort. It's no accident that I've repeated the word "effort" in three consecutive sentences (this being the third one), which some might consider a case of literary ineptitude. It is not—it's quite intentional. To point out that the process of development is never easy. It cannot be nice, pleasant, or relaxed either. That doesn't sound good, but in Latin— "*per aspera ad astra*"—much better. Especially for those who have made no effort to master this somewhat outdated language.

While praising development, it's a risky endeavor to inform the reader that it involves hardship, struggle, and exertion, not to mention challenges, troubles, obstacles, or other complications. It's not pleasing to the ear, or in the case of the written word, to the eye. It doesn't really help to add that once you get through the drudgery, there is a good chance of feeling some sort of satisfaction. On the other hand, I'm not going to flatter consumer taste forever. You've already bought the book, haven't you? So I would add that, along with effort, time is also essential for development. And plenty of it. How much? I'd say... an unlimited amount. You can evolve endlessly. No matter how smart you are, you can always increase your potential.

"What do you mean—endlessly?" I hear someone ask. "We live until we die, sometimes longer, sometimes not so long. If you're unlucky enough to run into a psychopath pedophile as a child while walking alone, it's even pretty short." Well, let me quickly correct one thing—we sometimes live longer, sometimes not so long. And to the pervert, I would add a health failure that could happen at any age. What else can be on the list? Burning engines, which tend to turn a flying plane into a not-so-flying one. It's also possible to belong to a nation temporarily in the wrong that is currently being slaughtered by another temporarily more right one (although the roles may reverse quite quickly). You can also drive a car that approaches one from the opposite direction that is driven by a guy who just had a heart attack, or who a few minutes earlier downed a bottle of vodka. For the sake of statistical decency, we shouldn't disregard venomous snakes, rabid dogs, lightning, earthquakes, and serial killers.

So the chances of multiplying one's potential during our earthly journeys aren't equal. Besides, it doesn't necessarily have to end with getting off the trail prematurely, to put it more poetically. Development comes with choices. Slaves, for instance, might have had a bit of an issue with this. And it wasn't temporary. This form of interpersonal relationship, once very popular, flourished over thousands of years. Actually, we don't need such harsh examples. Even the descendants of a monarch were subject to different privileges, depending on their order of arrival to this world. If we were to add children born out of wedlock into the mix, we can see additional rifts opening up. It would be hard to make a clear judgment on who had it better. Easy may prove to be more difficult, problems might end up being benefits, and the wind blowing straight into your face might just give you enough momentum. The bottom line is that conditions varied. Some might even complain that Nature was hardly just in that regard.

"O ye of little faith," I dare quote one of the evangelists. Unfortunately, I don't know which one... or whether the quote is correct at all. Anyway, I'm leaving it here because it sounds good and fits even better. Let me tell you this: everyone has similar opportunities for growth. It can't be any different. And if it were, it would make little sense. So I reject it because I have a deep faith in the sense. It's not even so much faith as observation and contemplation of events, as well as unbridled awe at how Nature designed everything.

Part V

HEAVENLY RULER(S)?

Chapter Eighteen

Since the dawn of time, people have felt that, unlike other living beings, "not on bread alone doth man live." I quote the evangelist again. This time I even managed to track him down. If you want to exercise your brain, you can try it too. People couldn't rid themselves of the impression that there is another reality beyond the earthly one, so they decided to develop in this direction just to find peace of mind. Eventually, the idea prevailed that there must be an omnipotent being—either singular or plural, depending on current trends and local preferences—who created everything and runs it all. The legitimate question of why it created and does run wasn't really pursued. This could have caused the recurrence of internal strife, and that's not what they had in mind.

This interpretation gained widespread approval and enjoyed great popularity among the peoples of Earth for many years. Only recently, when it turned out that lightning, the excessive voraciousness of certain insects, and the shaking of the ground weren't necessarily emanations of the bad mood of the heavenly ruler, have some people devised different concepts that completely deny the ruler's existence. At the same time—probably in order to seem more serious and remain consistent—in their revolutionary zeal they became skeptical about everything that doesn't smell of matter.

But let's not look too far into the future. Having resolved the duality of human nature and installed divine supremacy over themselves, people breathed a sigh of relief. Then they eagerly took to their favorite activity—which is making up stories. (And we're really good at it.) It's uncertain if they did it themselves or whether there were experts at work. Observing similar practices today, I would say it was the latter. The experts were people who knew the godly subject. It's not entirely clear where this knowledge came from. Perhaps, discerning the boom, the physically weaker yet more canny individuals sensed their chance and informed their slightly amazed companions that the Almighty had appeared to them in a dream and bestowed upon them their new mission. Or maybe—by coincidence, or thanks to their keen sense of observation and ability to foresee various events—they accurately predicted the eruption of a nearby volcano. This was credited to them as a connection to the higher power (I mean the heavens, not the volcano).

The appearance of different kinds of divine agents, such as priests, shamans, and other shepherds of souls, didn't necessarily involve insincere intentions. It was rather the result of the age-old rule of supply and demand. People felt more comfortable with intermediaries who seemed more knowledgeable in otherworldly matters. And the latter were happy, for one reason or another, to meet the need for new services. An expertise in native perennials and shrubs was helpful in filling the position of local sorcerer. After proper preparation, these plants were excellent in relieving a variety of ailments, as well as for sending competitors and troublemakers of any kind to the Other Side. The many attempts to obtain optimal blends were possibly combined with experimental tasting. This resulted in psychedelic trips and a better understanding of the Almighty's instructions. You could then pass them unto the little ones.

One of the world's leading religions suggests that God created man in his own image. I get the irresistible impression that it was exactly the other way around. People didn't only create divine beings. They also endowed them with very human traits, like susceptibility to flattery or the acceptance of bribery... which is quite easy to moan about, but what were they supposed to do? Sad to say, the deities had fits of rage from time to time. In addition, they possessed tremendous power and could do quite a lot of damage. So they had to be appeased every once in a while to make the cooperation more or less bearable. Today, we already know that frequent outbursts of anger can be the result of a number of medical conditions, such as *intermittent explosive disorder*, whatever that is. Our ancestors hadn't wised up to that yet, so they couldn't suggest a cure.

Instead, they sated the exuberant egos of their gods in every possible way. They brought them all kinds of goods, made sacrifices—slaughtered livestock or prisoners of war, erected buildings and monuments. All these activities were meticulously coordinated by a vigilant priestly frat. In the face of an oft-frustrated deity, half-assed efforts weren't an option. No one knows how many of the donated goods were actually transferred skyward and how many were used by God's servants themselves. Perhaps they kept hoarding the wealth to appease the deity on a rainy day. Who knows? Regardless of the proportion, being a spiritual guide became more and more popular of a career choice, garnering a lot of interest from applicants seeking a new profession.

The number of divine beings was also on the rise. One could even see a gradual specialization. There were gods of fire, water, forests, and meadows, of sea waves and mountain avalanches. Ancient Greeks dominated the competition, showing amazing inventiveness and creativity. They promoted dozens of deities, whose powers touched virtually every area. What's interesting, the Hellenes acted in a very modern way. They made sure not to discriminate against women and to maintain parity.

So there were male gods of war and of dead people—they should be listed exactly in that order. Female goddesses of youth, the hunt, and childbirth—listing them in this order also makes sense. Of vengeance and of the dawn—interestingly enough, women too. Of the sea—this time both sexes. Of the sun—he. Of the moon—she. Of the wind—he. The latter had four assistants. Each of them controlled different direction of gusts. Finally, there was a male god of wine—acceptable, given the parity of consumption. I found no mention of any assistants responsible for the white, red, and sparkling ranges.

Other nations also had the ambition to come up with their own supernatural beings, just as nowadays many countries enjoy having their national airlines, ready to pay through the nose on occasion in line with the very rational principle: "What, are we worse than these guys?!" While visiting foreign territories, not always for tourism, travelers not only pillaged and looted but also promoted their gods (and discredited local ones). Over time, priorities shifted. Spreading one's own beliefs became the official goal of trips to neighboring countries and overseas territories. It was artfully named "converting," meaning turning back or changing direction. This might suggest that those who needed to be converted had gone astray. It doesn't really make sense, does it? You can't stray from a road if you've never been on it in the first place.

Those who had gone off the rails usually knew nothing about the wrong direction, so they were somewhat surprised and not too keen on accepting this fact. This reluctance wasn't very well received by the visitors. They reacted with a variety of methods, ranging from gentle persuasion to the physical elimination of the most surprised individuals. (To be fair, the invaders would usually take good care of their remaining assets.) In their missionary zeal, they would often forget about the kind attitude toward their fellow men, a rule—or should I say suggestion—of one of the religions that was quite active in promoting itself. But the followers did so for the glory of God, which must have pleased the addressee. I'm sure he could turn a blind eye to the minor shortcomings.

There are also paradoxes in competing faith communities. One of them refers to the non-affiliated as nonbelievers—sometimes even advocating their extermination. This direction is especially en vogue in more radical circles. While calling for more restraint in the selection of targets, I'd also suggest cleaning up the nomenclature. I would limit the use of the term "nonbelievers" to people who reject all worship of supernatural beings. The others should be referred to as believers of a different or wrong kind.

Chapter Nineteen

Arguing about whether or not supernatural beings exist, and, if they do, which ones are more legitimate, is pointless. We keep trying to convince others of something, thereby neglecting ourselves in the process. If we were to critically examine our own views or beliefs, we might find, at least in some cases, that we are beginning to have some doubts. This would certainly weaken our enthusiasm for spreading personal concepts among other people in favor of perhaps attempting to first deal with the mess in our own heads. Leave others alone—they may be going through the exact same process and need to focus instead of dealing with your proselytizing.

When it comes to morality, there are no major discrepancies between the followers of different religions. The same is true for those who didn't enroll in any spiritual groups (or weren't enrolled as children). Some people raise concerns that without the fear of divine wrath, humankind would lose itself in the dark abyss of sin and vice. Even a cursory glance at reality doesn't confirm this far-fetched view. There are villains and decent men on both sides of the barricade.

The declaration of one's belief in supernatural beings or lack thereof should not matter either. If you've generally behaved decently during your earthly journey, you should enjoy the favor of a judge and jury at the final trial—even if you had previously denied the existence of such a body. Those who, in the absence of it, awaited the final judgment in vain, should equally not despair but quietly accept their ideological defeat. "*Errare humanum est,*" as the Roman speaker and writer used to say. To distinguish him from his famous descendant, he was referred to as the Elder.

Some more ardent believers might protest at this point. "Membership is highly relevant to the subsequent fate of the member!" I hear them cry. This reminds me of a conversation I once had with envoys of a certain evangelistic group. They promote their religion in a rather thankless manner, operating like traveling salespeople. They go from door to door and offer the good news—just like former competitors used to sell vacuum cleaners or meat grinders. Additionally, they are subjected to rather unsympathetic comments about harassing, spreading lies, or simply bugging people.

I'm a firm believer in learning about disparate points of view. Best to learn from the source. So I adopted a different strategy. I invited the weary missionaries in for a brief chat, offering refreshing liquids—like a good Christian would. After listening to them talk for a while, I tentatively suggested that maybe all one needs to do is apply the teachings of the Gospel in one's life, without having to wear any specific club colors. In return, I learned about the significant benefits of joining their particular guild. I have to admit that I didn't fully understand the offer. There was talk of some sort of hierarchy, privileges for members, higher floors (there's that hotel upgrade thing again), more comfortable chairs—something to that effect. Or perhaps I am wrong? I don't even know anymore.

When I recall that meeting, I can't help but think about how religions and travel agencies are somehow similar. The only difference is that the former offer only all-inclusive packages. And basically one destination. Everything had its beginning a long time ago. People started to analyze the surrounding reality. They considered it possible that some nonmaterial part of them doesn't die for good, but instead travels to the great Beyond. But what can you do to make sure you don't miss the trip? And how do you get there? If there is a demand, there is always a service provider. And the more interested customers, the richer the offer.

It took no time, and the vendors were mushrooming left and right. They assured that they had the right know-how on how to reach the destination reliably. At first, there were mostly individuals running something like a sole proprietorship. Over time, larger and larger corporations were founded, with offices and representatives all over the world. There was a steady increase in the number of agents, consultants, and the all-important marketing experts. Logistics hardly mattered in this case. The trip itself and the conditions were of no interest to the potential clientele.

The final destination, by contrast, strongly piqued the curiosity of prospective travelers, and so organizers pooled their ingenuity to develop this particular area. In addition to somewhat enigmatic descriptions that "eye hath not seen, nor ear heard," their offering also included more specific attractions. The angelic choirs were especially popular, followed closely by valleys filled with gorgeous flowers and heavenly music. There was also a meet-and-greet option, which offered an opportunity to interact directly and have a brief chat with local celebrities, like a gatekeeper of heaven or a supreme archangel.

Some offerings were addressed to a smaller audience. For specific achievements, such as blowing up the customers of competitors, the traveler would be awaited by a bunch of young women. This entertainment, however, was available solely to men. The ladies had virtually no experience with love conquests, which was considered a great boon for some reason.

In order to enjoy the attractions, you first had to sign up for the earthly loyalty program. It included a variety of activities, as well as fees. It was advisable to follow the terms and conditions. If you went astray (which happened rather frequently), you had the opportunity to repent. After a symbolic reprimand, you would resume your participation in the program. Those who couldn't make up their mind were not forgotten. Some hesitated because they couldn't decide which option to go for. Others had no idea that any option existed at all. Still others denied any journeys to the Other Side or were simply not interested. So a special last-minute offer had been devised for those who may have changed their mind at the last moment. This product was skillfully used by one of the two thieves, later referred to as the good one.

Finally, I'd like to mention another group of travelers. They prefer to prepare for the trip on their own. They get around and reach their destination in the same manner. This involves some effort and the risk of unexpected situations. On the other hand, it eliminates disappointment, when the reality proves to be nothing like the ads.

Chapter Twenty

When it comes to the belief in the afterlife, three trends remain the most common among Earthlings. Some claim that there is no existence after death. You die, and then... there's nothing. I'm not going to pay this proposal any further attention. Nothing means nothing, let's stay consistent.

Another group believes that at the end of our earthly life, we go to the Beyond, where we continue to exist, just by different rules. There are several suggestions of what that Beyond is supposed to look like. According to one, it consists of three areas: the great one, the awful one, and the something-in-between one. That's the first of them where the aforementioned angelic choirs and landscape wonders are located. Which area you end up in depends on your earthly conduct. So it seems worthwhile to put in some effort.

Those who end up in the awful zone are generally screwed. There's no way out. The realm is ruled by some supposedly horrid guys. Not only do they have many nasty characteristics, but they also take pleasure in being in rooms with very high temperatures. The lack of air conditioning doesn't bother them at all. Interestingly, they are exclusively male. I found no serious mentions of women holding any positions there. I wonder if the issue shouldn't be publicized somehow—it smacks of obvious discrimination. By the way, the same is true for the great zone. Except maybe the Virgin, but she just confirms the rule. This shares all the hallmarks of systemic pathology.

Most decedents end up in the something-in-between area. Their living relatives can make significant contributions to improving their lot (which is the transfer to the great area) through various interventions. It doesn't necessarily have to be family, by the way. Close or distant acquaintances and even complete strangers are also accepted—as long as they order some prayers. One-time prayers are fine, but getting a bundle is much better. One can also get their sins erased—this is known as an indulgence. All of these activities and boons usually require a payment of certain fees (lump sum or per treatment), but who would spare any expense to help their fellow man?

After a tedious earthly journey, the Beyond in its comfort version seems a desirable destination. Nevertheless, we seem to be quite sentimental when it comes to Earth. For this reason, a return is even envisaged in an unspecified future. Interestingly enough, in corporeal form at that. It will be combined with a re-audit and final evaluation of the earthly achievements of the returnees. The authors of this concept spare us the details, which is a pity, because some doubts inevitably arise.

The very issue of a new audit is already controversial. Could it be that the previous one had some margin of error? Also, would the new balance include everyone? Even those who've been in hellfire so far? What if it turns out someone ended up there by mistake? Would there be any compensation? Let's take a look at those who've been wallowing in heavenly comfort until this point. There's no denying they've become accustomed to it. What if they need to be demoted due to some rather shady things coming to light during the new audit? Can they appeal the decision, or would it be a lost cause?

The raising of the dead raises many questions as well. Or should we say "the return from the Beyond?" (This would definitely be better and more accurate wording.) Let me remind you, it also applies to our corporeal forms. I will leave aside the issue of overpopulation. What age are we going to be when we return to our bodies? If we go back exactly to the day we died, I wouldn't expect any particular enthusiasm. Especially among women who departed at a ripe old age. What about a child who succumbed to a nasty disease and had to say goodbye as an infant, while the parents passed away from old age? Who is going to take care of the baby? The elderly, ailing people? It would make sense to clarify some issues because the competition and the devil are out there and, as we know, they never sleep.

A third option for what happens beyond the grave also envisages the afterlife. In fact, it envisages many afterlives. The process of multiple travels is technically called "reincarnation." According to it, following one's death, you don't enjoy heavenly peace or grieve the lack of it, (depending on your behavior and assignment to a particular area). At least not indefinitely. After some time, you return to an earthly life and deal with the vicissitudes of fate once again. This idea carries a lot of charm and makes sense. I could end this description right here. But no, the human imagination and its irresistible desire to invent fanciful stories manifests itself in this case as well.

There are countless versions of what, why, when, and in what order. Their variety and the creativity of their authors is enough to make you dizzy. I didn't grow up in a geographical area dominated by the religions of the East, where reincarnation is doing best. My knowledge of this matter is based not on writings and treatises by sages who know this subject by heart, but from widely available sources. They tend to offer simplistic descriptions. Maybe that's why after a short while I got confused about what each option actually entails and what is offered by the various schools. So my further deliberations might be prone to a certain margin of inaccuracy. I'm pointing that out in case there are any experts on the subject among the readers, who might become annoyed or decide to enlighten me by sending correct interpretations.

The plethora of concepts comes from knowing reasonably well how to arrive at the truth. This prompts many people to make an attempt. You should indulge in intense thoughts, without thinking too much about anything. That gives you a good chance of getting into the areas that conceal the core and perhaps even reveal it. I'm a person who is open to new technologies. I also know that people say different things, but there is nothing like one's own experience. Which is why I decided to give it a try. Unfortunately, the results were hardly satisfactory—each time I fell asleep after just a brief moment. I was probably using the wrong technique. Or maybe I'm just not cut out for this stuff.

Depending on the version, the transition into a new state of being occurs either immediately or later down the line. There are even accurate estimates of how long the stopover might last. ("Accurate estimate" is a bit of a misnomer or even an oxymoron—you can either be accurate or you can estimate. Unless you've had a guess, and that guess was accurate.) One teaching suggests that the wait lasts forty-nine days. That is a little over a month and a half, so you can better imagine the timeframe. I haven't found any justification for this particular number. It doesn't matter, I wasn't that curious.

You can get into your next symbiosis with a new human being (some suggest other options, too). I'm not sure whether it concerns only newborns, or whether a freshly conceived person is also suitable, and if so, whether from the very beginning or later, and if later, when exactly. Either way, a human body as a new address is a favorable result. Those who don't limit the choice to just people also have nonmaterial entities in the catalogue. Celestial beings or demigods constitute decent outcomes. Hungry ghosts or hellish beings are... not so desirable. You can also end up as an animal, which is hardly a good option either.

When thinking about sacred cows, I was a bit taken aback by this seemingly uncalled for degradation of our animal brethren. Perhaps this is only a matter of various schools I keep mixing up due to my ignorance? I was even more surprised by the lack of a plant-based alternative. On the other hand, I think I can understand the authors' intentions, at least to some extent. We all have to eat something, and it wouldn't be a good idea to get stressed out about it because stress might lead to stomach ulcers. When eating meat, you typically know that it belongs to a decedent. Well, unless one has a taste for the living, but that's rare. The individual who was in symbiosis with an animal probably left it and started a new journey right as its throat was slit open. This essentially eliminates the risk of cannibalism.

In the case of plants, determining their death can be more troublesome. Back in the day, I used a stick to support a potted shrub. It was a cutoff from a potted palm tree that had long withered. To make the support effective, I pressed it into the soil where the shrub grew. After a while, the stick came to life and sprouted its own leaves. So it's not entirely clear whether we're eating living plants when we consume lettuce or carrots. It may also be the case for parsley (both cut and root), as well as beets, leeks, or celery.

With this in mind, I can better understand excluding flora from the equation. All the more so when you remember that oaks, sequoias, or other baobabs, after taking hold or, rather, rooting properly, can live on for millennia. They don't even consider falling over. And if they would (consider), people would prop them up or pour concrete around them because we like big numbers, hardly caring about the unfortunate soul linked to the tree in an unpleasant symbiosis. For some animals, the time perspective can also be daunting. Coexistence with, say, a polar shark means 270 years of cold bathing. Or even longer—some sources claim they live for as long as 392 years. Let me ask: How about 360? Or 403 and a half? As always with numbers, proceed with caution. Nothing can beat the scholarly imagination and their passion for fairy tales.

Where we dock in the next life depends on the conduct in the present one. (You've probably noticed some overlapping with the competitors, who offer only one-way tickets.) A virtuous man has a good chance of not becoming a hungry ghost, hellish being, or crocodile. He will most likely become another person. But what kind? Does a good incarnation mean a symbiosis with somebody better off financially? Some say that money doesn't make you happy. But if assets matter, what then? The more the better? Or worse, if you exceed a certain amount? What if it were the other way around? Are we then talking about abject poverty, or just some financial struggle?

The number of trips to the Beyond is also unspecified. There may be many; in the less optimistic outlook, maybe even an awful lot. The goal is for them to end. This happens when you immerse yourself in the absence of thought so intensely that you reach understanding, opening up the gates to a better dimension... Or something like that. Our stays on Earth are not considered good situations. We face them without knowing why. Maybe the Creator wanted to see if we were going to make it? If not, it meant we were deemed unworthy. The question is why he wanted to check it out in the first place. As an omniscient being, he must have known we wouldn't make it. Alternatively, he could've improved us a bit. But then he'd know we would make it, so he wouldn't have to check it out. Well, the Lord works in mysterious ways.

Part VI

THE SOLUTION

Chapter Twenty-One

Human memory is fallible, so it's not a bad idea to refresh it from time to time: "The driving force behind all processes occurring in Nature is the urge to evolve. It is an ongoing process of interactions and verifications. It creates new structures, improves existing ones, or destroys them if the checks fail. This scheme guarantees the best possible outcome and further optimal development. It concerns every form of matter, as well as humans."

I'd also like to remind you of the existence of natural forces. They define the rules of the Game of Development. They are fixed, unchanging, and indifferent. They don't give a damn whether we like them or not. There is no way to beg, manipulate, or bribe them. Neither by hook nor by crook. It doesn't matter who is trying—a supernatural being or not-so-supernatural man.

Non-living matter changed, forming new structures from the available building materials. Two atoms of hydrogen and one of oxygen made water. It came in very handy. The strategic goal was reaching a state where life could thrive. It worked here on Earth. No one tinkered with it, but it wasn't a complete accident either. It had to work out that way at some place sooner or later. The matter reached the desired state, which ensured access to another force, as implacable and incorruptible as the previous ones, only more powerful.

Living organisms evolved in widely different ways. They had access and could replicate themselves, which they did with might and main. This came in very handy. The strategic goal was to generate an individual who would have access to another force—just as unrelenting and incorruptible as the previous ones, only even more powerful—and to new and immeasurable resources. Nonmaterial and exorbitant. It was a long process that encompassed innumerable attempts on many fronts—in the water, air, and on land, where, eventually, it worked out. A human came to existence. No one tinkered with it, but it wasn't a complete accident either. It had to work out that way at some point. Sooner or later.

That's what I believe—and why, I specified on previous pages. I have no desire to repeat myself—I'm not being paid per word or sentence. If you don't remember or you read inattentively, feel free to go back and reread the content. This isn't a disposable text or some fruity chew. If you disagree or have a different opinion (which is more or less the same), that's your sacred right. You are invited to argue with me. I dare say, I advise you to do so. Of course, terms and conditions apply. Left pocket and right pocket are only good when it comes to clothing, and beating around the bush might be an adequate gardening practice but not so great with regard to debates.

I qualify the arguments about the chaotic stirring occurring in Nature as beyond their "best-by" date and unfit for mental consumption. The same goes for conclusions involving some tinkerer, who tampered with the events out of passion or any other reason. Before you present your own version and claim its superiority (which can't be ruled out), you should first constructively destroy mine, preferably by exposing its shortcomings and presenting strong arguments proving that I'm spouting bull. I mean strong, so please don't use some wishy-washy suspicions or claims, or point out inconsistencies with the dogmas of Science, the Holy Inquisition, or other sources of Truth. I look forward to your rational criticism. Best regards, author. In the meantime, I'll go on with my deliberations.

People are the inevitable consequence of the developmental processes occurring in Nature. They continue to evolve, only at a higher level compared to their predecessors. I can't imagine what other reason we would take up space on Earth for. If I'm right, one biological lifetime is clearly not enough for decent development. Especially when you remember that our starting positions are very different. Imagine a 100-meter run. The blocks of the first sprinter are exactly where they belong, the second a little closer to the finish line, the third even closer, and so on. The chances of success now mainly depend on drawing the right track, while persistence and training become less important. The situation would change radically if there were multiple runs with every possible runner-track configuration, and all results were summed up (we assume the weather was identical all the time).

The same is true for life expectancy, which may also vary. Since the athletic analogy above seems to be working, I will go for one more. This time everyone starts from the same place, but the finish line is at a different point for every competitor. Again, doing multiple runs would level the playing field… but only at first glance. If you, dear reader, have been fooled by my deft sport parallels, don't worry. You are not the first and certainly won't be the last.

I mean, what if one of the runners is wearing seven-mile boots? Regardless of how far his finish line is, he's going to win every time. Besides, the boots weren't actually seven-mile, but seven-league ones. A league, which fell out of favor as distance measurement some time ago, amounted roughly to three miles. So we speak de facto of twenty-one-mile boots. That means moving even faster and winning by a much larger margin. Plus setting a new world record. If anyone doubts the existence of such shoes, a certain Charles Perrault didn't just mention them. He also described their various uses and benefits. For those who still have their doubts, I'll fire an even higher caliber: Goethe, *Faust*, Part Two.

It could also be the other way around. Suppose one of the runners had done a bit of mischief in the past. As a result, he is currently spending his time in a high-security penitentiary. However, because of his former athletic achievements, he is admitted to some competitions (in compliance with the necessary precautions, of course). So he moves on the track with his legs chained together or tied with a cable clip. The rest of the sprinters, in their seven-league boots, run-of-the-mill shoes, or no sneakers at all, would quickly disillusion him about getting a good result. Unless they tried running in cement shoes. This kind of footwear, however, is more common in cross-country routes running along the shore of a body of water.

The mention of cement shoes wasn't just a clever yet unexpected punchline of the previous paragraph. The next bit is going to be about death. Yes, again. I needed a neat transition, and cement shoes fit the theme, just like paper ones. I'd like to add that you put neither of them on yourself. Either you don't want to or aren't able to. The first are donned while the cadaver-in-the-making is still alive. Otherwise their use, considering the complex logistics and noticeable material usage, wouldn't make much sense. A bag, heavy stone, and piece of rope would suffice.

When it comes to death, I have good news. In Nature, it's not the end of the road—at least not for those who make an effort and move in the right direction. No, this isn't just dumb propaganda or a new advertising slogan to further polish the image. (Besides, I never did get paid for the previous presentation. I should probably send my invoice. Does anybody know the address?) An animal or a plant—the ones reared by humans don't count—usually has time to reproduce before it dies or withers. This means that its development goes on, only in an updated version. The end of life doesn't stop this process. It only eliminates what can no longer develop.

People also evolve during their lifetime, just one floor higher. It's not about honing the genetic material. The issue is no longer claws, beaks, or even brains. We don't continue to evolve through our offspring. If that were the case, I—being a fisherman—would have a fisherman father. A fisherman would also be his father—and my grandfather. Same with my grandfather's father—my father's grandfather and my great-grandfather. And the next father, who would be my grandfather's grandfather, my father's great-grandfather and my great-great-grandfather. The offspring, born to me and the daughter of some other fisherman, would be fishermen as well. At least until there was a shortage of fish in the waters. My son would be a fisherman, as would his son—and my grandson, as well as my grandson's son—my son's grandson, and my great-grandson. And it's not a matter of ten or fifty generations, should someone of noble origin want to protest, bringing up his family tree. Let me remind you of the anteater and the fifty million years, or rather an awful lot.

The process of your development, though it no longer takes place in your genes or offspring, is also incessant. Death leaves you be. And if someone still nitpicks on the matter of genes: "How is that? Don't we pass them on?" Sure, but that occurs along the way. The main process takes place elsewhere. Or it doesn't—depending on what you prefer and choose. Below, I'll offer a simple solution, how a man can persist and develop without being bothered by death, with a guarantee of equal opportunities for everyone: white, cream, copper, or black (or in reverse order, if that would suit you better—some read right-to-left anyway). The guarantee also covers the historical moment, geographical location, financial and social status, more or less crazy parents, membership in the slaughtered/slaughtering group, a pervert one meets as a child, burning plane engines, and a drunk driver coming from the opposite direction. Nice bundle, isn't it? No way anyone's going to trump me.

Chapter Twenty-Two

If we strip the concept of reincarnation of the various embellishments and ornaments tacked onto it with creative zeal over the centuries, it turns out to be a very clever idea. I wonder who came up with it and how it happened? I imagine a logically thinking fellow, who once, while contemplating the nature of things or humans, suggested a simple form of re-existence. However, he underestimated the creative potential of his successors, who—probably anticipating the power of this solution—decided to add some extra watts, unfortunately forgetting about moderation in the process.

This reminds me of another noble man. At one time he wandered around Galilee, promoting his own ideas. Not really complicated ones, either. It was mainly about treating other people with due respect based on the way people treat themselves, plus some odds and ends about multiplying one's talents, the camel and the eye of the needle, or letting go of fear. This letting go he practiced personally, which eventually got him in trouble—but maybe principles are more important? It's not entirely clear where, when, and why he did or said what he is said to have done or said. His followers also went off on tangents and expanded upon his teachings to quite an astounding extent. Neglecting moderation again. Well, history does tend to repeat itself.

To grow, you have to put forth effort. This generally leads to discomfort but is worthwhile because, in the end, the outcome is very satisfactory. This sequence keeps repeating. After getting satisfaction, you want the next installment. To get it, you have to make another effort. Satisfaction is a bonus that you evolved. Otherwise, you might be unwilling to try. You are even more willing when you know that the playing field is level, there is no corruption, nepotism, or turning of a blind eye. No juggling, manipulation, or other monkey business. This game has clear rules, which are unchangeable and apply to everyone. There are no bents, biases, fondnesses, inclinations, leanings, partialities, penchants, predilections, preferences, proclivities, sympathies, or tastes. No likes, dislikes, and the like.

We live and develop on Earth, not in heaven. There aren't problems there so how are you supposed to grow? It would be nice to participate in the process all the time. That would be only fair. A fellow who lived back in the day mostly dug holes into which mammoths or saber-toothed tigers fell (or not). He had less intellectual leeway than you, dear reader, if I may accost you and compare. So let's assume you were also there at the time, possibly in a different area.

How could it have gone, you and the mammoth pit? Let me introduce you to Robert. He is a lesser-known colleague of Adam. I chose him so as not to be accused of favoring celebrities. Robert was receiving his impulses (he happily didn't ignore them) and established his connection to the new dimension. Then he developed a part of his nonmaterial assets. It wasn't that big, but still. He managed to do this before he fell in battle with a saber-toothed tiger. The pit was too shallow, and Robert too slow. I'm fantasizing a little. When Robert was at that stage, he didn't know that it was possible to dig a hole for something (or even for someone, but that came much later).

The connection was severed. Robert quickly made a new one. He could once again enjoy the sunshine, the sound of the wind, and the chirping birds. As well as hate lightning bolts, heavy rain, and intrusive female mosquitoes. He was a little surprised because his name was no longer Robert—he was now called Emil. The neighborhood seemed somewhat unfamiliar, too. However, he quickly got used to it, especially since he couldn't remember Robert, anyway. If he could, he might have been even happier. Previously his back was killing him, his teeth had lost their enamel, and his hair had faded white (the remaining teeth and hair, I mean). Now he had a brand-new body, and tons of new attractions were waiting for him—as well as new issues. But he hardly worried about that because he was bursting with energy. In addition, something told him (maybe Robert) that he would make it all right. He only had to outrun the tiger this time.

And so it goes, my dear reader. Perhaps former Robert and Emil, or Roberta and Emily, as well as… honestly, no idea, that's a lot of names to remember. So it goes, and so it's going to go for a long time…

I can imagine that more sensitive readers might want to take a short break here. So let's change the discipline for a moment. What is 2,000,000 or two million, divided by 50 or fifty? (I write both numbers and words because I don't know what everyone prefers, and I recently have read on a wall "don't leave anyone behind." I need to take care of all my readers. After all, the book costs the same for everyone.)

I won't reveal the result of the division right away. I'll give those who want to try a chance. At least to turn on a calculator. A piece of paper and pencil are obviously better, but even they hardly compare to a mental workout without the use of aids. Okay, time's up. If you didn't get the answer, don't worry—you'll have another opportunity in a moment. The quotient (the proper name for the result of a division, in case you didn't know) is 40,000 or forty thousand. Now, let me raise the stakes a bit. Divide 2,000,000,000 or two billion, or an awful lot, by 100 or one hundred. I'll give you a small hint—just cut off two zeros, and there you have your answer. You're right, the second result is 20,000,000 or twenty million, which is basically also an awful lot, just a slightly smaller one.

Now let's compare both quotients and find out how much of the second is the first. Hardly a large value. I'd even say it's very small. I mention it just to give those who are up for a math challenge some more time. So let me add that right now it's raining heavily outside, and this is a change compared to the previous day, since we had beautiful weather here. Some call it a breakdown. Interestingly, it doesn't break down in reverse, it just breaks. From the point of view of plants, both situations are desirable. Perhaps we should be talking about a nice switch instead of a breakdown? Maybe the combination of both phenomena would be best. It doesn't happen very often, and when it does, there's a rainbow in the sky.

Done with the math yet? The answer is 0.2% or two-tenths of one percent. In case someone doesn't know what I'm talking about, it's 2‰ or two per mille, or two thousandths of something. If the trouble persists, take this something, divide it into a thousand equal parts, then separate two parts from the rest. Just a little, you can see the difference right away. Now, suppose a person lives on average 101 years. I'm exaggerating a bit, but the number will look nice in further calculations. Besides, we can't rule out that it's going to be accurate one day. Two per mille of that would be a seventy-four-day-old baby, interchangeably two and a half months old, if the child was born on February 1st on a non-leap year. Our imaginary 101-year-old also couldn't have been born in a leap year. Otherwise, the whole elaborate calculation goes down the drain.

A more inquisitive reader would probably be curious to know what all these numbers mean. And what the author intended with the calculations. Let's not kid ourselves—this wasn't just about cooling down emotions or taking a technical break.

Two million is the number of years since Adam received his first impulse and kickstarted the journey of humanity. Maybe it was a little earlier, maybe a little later. No one knows exactly, and no one will ever know. But don't worry, this knowledge isn't useful for anything. It's not some wild number, like ten thousand or 800 million. Even if it's off by a million or two, it hardly matters in terms of global accounts. I'll prove it in a minute.

Fifty also represents the number of years. It's the average lifespan of a person who lived somewhere along the mentioned two million. I'm overestimating again, but it's easy to divide, so everyone has a chance. Besides, I can always use other values. I recently unearthed fresh bones (I mean, not exactly fresh, they just came from another hole), did some additional studies, and conducted new experiments. It turned out that the first impulse occurred 1 million 520 thousand years ago, and the average lifespan was thirty-eight years. I divide, it's still forty thousand—the total number of life cycles, starting with Adam (or Robert) to this day.

How much time do we have left on Earth? This is a perfect field for experts to maneuver. I'm not very familiar with the subject at hand, but I will make a wager, counting on the beginner's luck. Two billion years, give or take. This amounts to 24 billion months, 730 billion 400 million days, or 17 trillion 529 billion 600 million hours. Let's subtract 5 trillion 843 billion 200 million hours—there's nothing like getting a good night's sleep. If you dislike sleeping in, feel free to change the value. There are 11 trillion 686 billion 400 million hours remaining to be used. Imagine that there are people who say they don't have time.

I assumed that the average life expectancy in the future would be 100 years. I beg your pardon? What, 101? Oh, right. Meanwhile, living conditions deteriorated, lowering the average. Besides, sometimes numbers can be fudged just to get a nice result. I'm not the first, and definitely not the last. And that concludes our math class for today. All the numbers should be clear by now. If not, you know what to do. There are 20 million cycles available, which is 99.8% of all possible. We've used only 0.2% to date—pretty much nothing. May I recall the two-and-a-half-month-old infant? It's got lousy manners, shits in a diaper, and makes slurred noises. You were also like that, dear reader. Look at you now, all grown up!

Chapter Twenty-Three

If you play dice, you know—you don't have much control. No matter how flexible is your wrist, how nimble are your fingers, and how expensive is the leather your cup is made of, every cast is left to chance. But if you show patience, throwing, say, 20 million 40 thousand times, you're going to get all the possible combinations. Sooner or later, in this order or another, but for certain and repeatedly. Five-of-a-kind is the best outcome. All fours, ones, or others—doesn't matter. Bum is the opposite, such as 12456 when you need threes. Both five-of-a-kind and bum are rare, but bum happens to be less rare. Usually it's a little better or worse, sometimes not bad or not really. It can also be fairly okay. The opposites are excellent or disastrous. These too are opposites, only bigger.

While each turn and the outcome are purely left to chance, what happens next is the decision of the player. After the dice are cast, you might just want to mention it, indicating the inevitability of the events to come, like a certain Roman emperor once did. You can also lean thoughtfully over the numbers, contemplating what to do with them next. This requires some effort. Contemplating, that is. Leaning doesn't involve any substantial struggle, which makes it unworthy of mention. Of course, taking a break is always an option.

You can kick back, have some beer, then cast the dice again without any reflection. It may happen, though, that the chance is missed and the next turn gives you a bum.

I mention this game not because I'm a dice aficionado. I hardly play any board games, and if I do, then it's usually for money (at reasonable rates). I just find in this relaxing activity an amazing analogy to how Nature works. I know, Cousin Albert suggested that God doesn't play dice with the world, but I need to denounce the ancestor for the first time, even though I would personally prefer to keep the Almighty out of the game. A little later, Einstein wrote that the Creator does cast the dice but on his own terms. That sounds a little better. I would just suggest the dice be cast by the thrower. There's no need to burden God's hand.

Did I mention that I sometimes also play bridge? So, for those who can't keep up with my colorful run-math-baby-dice metaphors and allegories, let me lay my cards on the table. The meaning of human existence is development. This process is ongoing, and everyone can participate. How far you get depends on how much effort you are willing to put forth. You don't vanish into nothingness or, if you will, die. This only happens to your consecutive biological packaging. You instead grapple with fate all the time. We've been doing this since we were making fire and digging mammoth pits, and it's continued through driving a car to... many other activities. Before you ask—no, I have no idea what we're going to do in the distant future. Perhaps... make fire? To keep it fair (as is always the case in Nature) and give everyone the same opportunities, we find ourselves in a different random situation every single time. Here today, gone tomorrow; one time riding a horse in the saddle, another time bareback (or with no horse at all). There can be many of these times, and you need to face any option.

What do we develop? That's something you need to decide for yourself. After all, you're the one who's going to take care of it. It's best to listen to your own advisers, such as instinct, experience, or inner voice. The external ones can talk all sorts of crap, although they don't necessarily have to. We generally can sense what is important and what isn't. That's always a clue. There are also concepts such as virtues or morals. This seems to be the right direction. It's good to remember that you are going to encounter very different situations. What's useful in each of them is exactly what's going to be valuable as well. If you currently own a large amount of earthly goods, such as stocks, land, or paintings by great masters (or just smears that for some reason hold a high market value), the ability to accumulate them may not necessarily be useful in the next episode. But courage? Very much so. It's very helpful in business dealings, anyway.

Finally, it's important to keep in mind that other people sometimes want to develop too. You shouldn't hinder them. On the other hand, by hindering, we do give them additional opportunities to grow—assuming that they're willing to exert even more effort. But we waste time and neglect our own development. So to balance things out, don't hinder others. That's roughly it. Get to it, dear reader, if you want to take advantage of the promise from the title. As for me... again, I feel this strong urge to stop writing at this point. No way. When you encourage others to do something—say, to make an effort—it's not bad to set an example yourself. Is your own business done? So many questions are piling up, dear author.

Changes in non-living matter had a purpose. The development of life. The evolution of living organisms also had a purpose. That's us. What strategic thought guides the development of humans? Is this just the next step? And if so, what is the purpose of it? And what happens after that? Like I said before, if you don't know, just say it out loud. Consider it done. It's like expecting an owl—this animal is widely regarded to be wise—to know that it was ultimately about us. Besides, who on earth could have guessed that the apes would be the closest? This reminds me of La Fontaine's famous fable... The important thing is, we know what we need to focus on in the meantime. So, stop gathering wool—just roll up your sleeves and evolve.

Another question could be about proportion. I can already hear some math enthusiast yell from the back: "Wait, wait, something's wrong here! Too much flesh, too little spirit!" He's probably referring to the ever-increasing human population, a trend that has picked up pace in the last century. A simple calculation would show that some of us—most of us, in fact—don't have any particular past to boast of (or to be ashamed of). Who said we need to? Just because you have access doesn't mean you've taken advantage of it. Take a look at the crowds fighting their way through the store doors on the very dark fifth day of the week (at the end of November). Once inside, they push each other around and fight for the best take. Like flocks of cattle driven across the steppes or a pack of wolves tearing apart a bagged moose. Someone's evolving, and someone may not have started yet because he missed the signal or jammed it.

While the analogy is fine, this remains its only virtue. It does nothing to dispel the doubts of our mathematician. Let's then assume that some people are just taking the first steps on their journey. This is not that big of a handicap—99.8% of the trip is still ahead of us! An infant, after living for less than three months, doesn't have much to show off yet (even if the parents strongly disagree). And the size of the world population, if current trends continue, will begin shrinking before long. If anybody doubts this, just check out the mouse experiment. It was about eliminating all problems from the rodents' lives. I'll give it a bit more attention later in the book, but it might do you good to prepare for the lecture and explore the topic in advance.

The people coming from more prosperous countries with strongly developed labor privileges might want to throw in another question. "What about vacation days? If you keep pushing others to grow and make efforts, you should also tell them when they will be able to rest." If I understand that question correctly, it's about swinging in the clouds between one episode and the next. Unfortunately, once again, I have no idea, and I'm running out of visions. If I had to guess, I'd wager a small amount on "no vacation." Despite the duality of human nature, man's place is on Earth. I can't imagine what we could do in the heavens that would be useful. Besides, who would determine if and when the holiday is over? The participants themselves? I can already see people frolicking in the skies, chastising themselves for their unwillingness to continue grappling with fate (and then, overcome with remorse, quickly packing up their stuff and setting off on another journey). Who am I kidding? So, no vacation days. Actually, we'll just have to wait (or rather die) and see. And I still politely remind you of free will. If you prefer, you can also laze around on Earth.

Chapter Twenty-Four

Proponents of reincarnation based on religious beliefs suggest that people's subsequent fates depend on karma. I hope I'm interpreting correctly. Karma is a balance sheet of past lives, to employ an accounting metaphor. The better the result, the more favorable the outlook gets, just like in business. I couldn't quite figure out who is conducting the audit and managing the future fate. There's a bunch of experts, and each of them is pushing their own version. You have several religions, with even more currents, schools, and branches.

The overall direction is quite consistent. Good behavior means better conditions in the next life. Each of them is like a stay in prison anyway, the next might only be a lower-security one. What better terms entail in reality? No idea. More money? An easier job? Perhaps both? Putting the irony aside (I'm finding it very difficult), it's all about simple and easily digestible promises to improve the lot of oppressed people. They swallow it thankfully, even if it is all pie in the sky. A prospect of an upgrade to the higher class is always welcome. Nothing has changed in this regard for millennia.

I propose a slightly different concept of reincarnation. It's based more on observation and analysis of the phenomena occurring in Nature, rather than on visions by various gurus and prophets (and their different interpretations). I'd like to emphasize that I'm unsure whether I'm copying something, some secret meanings or intentions. I wasn't allowed to comprehend many verses. "A real and, in the ultimate sense, true and definitive understanding of karma is only possible through a deep insight into the Impersonality and Causality of all phenomena of existence." Sorry, I don't dig it, no matter how hard I try. It sounds remarkably like some scientific passages. "Two centrioles involved in telophase of mitosis and meiosis are located in the cytoplasm." I particularly love the telophase. I looked it up and I already know that it's the process where "the daughter chromosomes arrive at the spindle poles and are eventually redistributed into bulk chromatin."

I'll call my version of multiple existences *natural*—just for the sake of clarity. This adjective is naturally derived from Nature. You can consider the name Natural Reincarnation reserved. I'm not going to trouble patent offices because I believe in human decency. Actually, that's not true, so I change my motivation to "because I don't feel like it," which is as true as it gets. The next distinction is about the absence of the pie in the sky. No matter how big a paragon of virtue you are in your current life, the dice don't care. In the next one, you may roll a bum. Or five-of-a-kind. And most likely, they'll land something in between. You can never rule out a bum, though. Which could make someone quite indignant: "Why the hell did I work so hard, persistently pursue my goals, stubbornly go to such great lengths, strenuously put forth so much effort, patiently try to be patient, help a blind old lady get across the street —all just to end up in a maximum security jail now?"

The effort wasn't in vain, if that helps. Quite to the contrary. If you get a bum, your qualities will help you face the misery and emerge victorious from the struggle with fate. It doesn't have to be financial destitution, by the way. There are much worse variations. You could end up becoming a subhuman among strangers, or even among your own kind. You might land in some crazy cult. Or just get parents who are screwed up. In a difficult situation, it's easier to falter if you've never had to wrestle with destiny. You're sure to roll a bum sooner or later—get ready for it in advance. Natural verification can be brutal because the standards are quite high. If you don't meet them, you know where you are going to end up. Of course, you can get all offended and depressed. The only problem is that Nature doesn't care—no matter how strong the headache, how overwhelming the weakness, and how hard it gets. So, to battle, dear reader. If it's any consolation, I also have some good news—two bums in a row happen very rarely.

Bum, five-of-a-kind, or something else; I wonder when the dice are going to be cast again. Not that I'm particularly interested in it, but you can let your imagination run a little wild, just for exercise. I would also be dumb not to imagine that someone would want to speculate on this topic. I prefer to do it myself, all while seeking moderation and keeping in check our passion for inventing tall tales. The end of the episode seems obvious. The biological shell dies, the connection is offline... Or something like that. Technology doesn't matter in the slightest. If there's no vacation, and let's assume there isn't, the access gets active and the first free person can (or must) take it.

To maintain proper research integrity, let me mention that on average four people are born every second in the world (data from about 2020 AD). Two people die at the same time. You don't need to be a mathematician to see that more people are being born. Which would indicate there's not enough for everyone. Roughly for half of the current population. Wrong. There's enough for everyone and even many more. There's not enough of previously used ones, but that's hardly an issue—remember the 99.8%? It seems that about one in two uses private access, so to speak, and one in two takes advantage of OA (open access). This is of course nothing but a simulation with a huge margin of error. Not everyone had to create their own account. They might have been too lazy to do that, for example. This would lead to a lower number of private users—not every one in two people, but one in ten, twenty-seven, or even one in two hundred and thirty-four.

So the access was activated. After a moment, dear reader, you've become someone else. I mean, not exactly—you're still you, only in a different skin. You have to learn to talk again. Even before that, you'll need to relearn how to maintain an upright posture and master movement. But there's no reason to despair. Your limbs are young and eager to learn. It's much worse when you reach adulthood. When a stroke strikes you (okay, your neighbor) and suddenly takes away speech along with movement, it's much more difficult to regain former performance. So, rejoice for now and embark on a new journey.

By the way, it would be really exciting to watch the draw of the new incarnation. Experience the thrill of the moment—whose skin will you get this time? I can already see bookies assessing possible configurations of gender, complexion, geographic coordinates, social status, or wealth. Perhaps we could even launch a new type of gambling outlet. Or at least turn it into a popular reality show or a TV series. Alas, I have to tame my imagination. Even though the software is already fairly advanced, the hardware is still in its infancy. It will take some time before it can take full advantage of the apps. If you're confused and have no idea what I'm on about, that's okay. You haven't missed anything important.

Let me still cool down the enthusiasm of the computer maniacs unnecessarily agitated by my digital allegory. It was just a nice metaphor, nothing more. I decided to weave it in because it fits fairly well and because I could. Unlike artificial and lifeless intelligence, as well as all sorts of chips, microprocessors, and other circuit boards. And no matter how hard you try, how many clever theories you come up with, how big or small the numbers you use, how many proteins you can culture and genes you transplant—no way, it's not going to happen. If you don't see the difference between a stone, a turtle, and a soldier in a trench with only his helmet sticking out... Well, Nature doesn't care about your views. It only cares about the merits. Do whatever you can before they are verified.

When does the connection resume? At conception seems a bit premature. The only organ capable of communicating still needs a while. Maybe there's some kind of pre-booking or first-come, first-serve principle? Any further debate, whether it's the fourth, seventh, or ninth month, is completely pointless. How about the twelfth day after birth? Or the fiftieth? "I have fifty, looking for fifty-five, anybody with fifty-five?" Nope. I'm canceling the auction. Maybe everyone's ready at a different time? While this sounds reasonable, it's also meaningless. Someone might just as reasonably suggest that since the consideration is superfluous, perhaps the entire paragraph should face a similar fate. To which I say that I respectfully disagree. The point is not to get too bogged down in the details. First, that's where the devil dwells and we wouldn't like to meet him. Secondly, the *what* is usually more important than the *how*.

One thing needs to be clarified, though. Whether a future human being has a brain or not (temporarily), doesn't put him into different categories. This is not a criterion when someone's considering prematurely ending a new life for these or other reasons. Sometimes it's determined by biology and other times by human choice. The decision is left to the chooser, more precisely to the female one. That's how Nature arranged it. As a member of the opposite sex, I know nothing in this regard. I can't use any intuition, instinct, or experience. I'm not going to mix logic into this either. I don't see the point. Besides, even if I were a woman, I would only have my own data to feed from. Belonging to the same sex changes little in this respect. I would bring this to the attention of the most militant female fighters on both sides of the barricade.

Chapter Twenty-Five

I introduce the concept of Natural Reincarnation not in order to convince anyone. If you've missed the subject—perhaps while reading this book on the train you took a nap, lulled by the clatter of the wheels—let me remind you that I propose a cyclical existence in successive incarnations. They're completely random. They don't depend in any way, shape, or form on your conduct in previous lives. This guarantees a natural tendency toward development and equal opportunities for all. This is, of course, if you have faith in probability theory. The only person I'd like to successfully infect with this idea is myself—but in the future because now I know. Though if I know now, I should know it later, even if conditions were much worse. Which I'll find out anyway, admittedly without knowing that I've found out.

However, if for some reason I wouldn't know, I'm sharing the notion just in case. I have no idea where I will end up and how to make sure that I will be familiar with the concept. A publicly available book at an affordable price seems to be a reasonable option. I won't be aware that I wrote it; I won't be able to take advantage of its popularity either. But there's nothing stopping me from writing another, creating beautiful paintings, or turning individual notes into wistful or sprightly tunes. I might also build a bridge over troubled water with companions or carve a tunnel into a mountainside...

To what extent can the assets accumulated in our present life be useful in the next one? It depends on which values we are thinking about. The ability to mend socks or human entrails; great command of a tongue, expressed by writing poetry or licking honey from a jar; proficiency with a scythe at harvest, a bow when playing violin, or a brush when painting a kitchen or landscape; the mastery to juggle legal acts or torches in the circus; kicking, punching, tossing, throwing, and pushing objects, as well as other people, while taking part in sports competitions... if I were to venture a guess, I'd say it's all subject to transport restrictions. There's also no shipping, courier, luggage room, or self-storage. So... everything's lost, right?

Not exactly. We also collect more universal values. Or at least some of us do. They seem to be useful in all situations. They are—in alphabetical order, so that I'm not accused of any bias—courage, diligence, honesty, moderation, modesty, patience, perseverance, reliability, tolerance. And a few others we know all too well. I'd wager they could get through the security line without a hitch. They constitute our indestructible capital and determine a person's worth—unlike a fat wallet, a fancy car, or a bunch of dumb followers. This doesn't mean that you can only have one or the other. Most wealthy people are courageous, hardworking, and persistent. As for other virtues... well, it varies. One can find it hard to resist temptations, especially when the ego gets its way.

What of the qualities that don't enjoy a good reputation? What about greed, laziness, and cowardice? I'm afraid they need to be packed as well. In your future journey you'll face them and struggle with them again. Keep in mind that the laws of Nature are merciless. Based on the evolutionary experience of living beings, it seems that most of them have failed to stand the test of time. Whether this also holds true for humans? I wouldn't exclude that possibility because the same rules of the game apply to us as well.

So I'd be on my guard just in case. If you don't believe it or think otherwise—that's your business and your choice. You have every right to exercise that choice. Let me only remind you that it doesn't matter what anyone thinks. Nature is as it is. It doesn't care about your views, no matter how passionately you express them. Imagine someone intoxicated by alcohol or some other agent disturbing his senses, or crushed by the worries of everyday life (or both crushed and intoxicated), standing at the edge of a cliff. After a while, more or less consciously, he takes a step forward. It's irrelevant what opinion he has about the direction, speed, and subsequent parameters of his further movement. He may believe in gravity or deny its existence. It has no bearing on the outcome.

"And what is this Nature?" I hear you ask, and I can feel you're slightly annoyed by the constant references. I could suggest careful observation and analysis of the surrounding reality, combined with letting your imagination run wild. But I feel like this isn't going to help with your stress—quite the opposite. So I'll give you an alternative. Nature is a set of eternal and unchanging laws, rules, and forces that affect the existence of all reality and the processes within it. I'm not going to go for a more precise description. As I've mentioned before, I don't experience visions. I only take hallucinogens in liquid form and in moderation. As long as they have enough volume, when heavily diluted. In an attempt to answer your question before you ask: I have no idea where these laws, rules, and forces came from. I'd wager that no one established them. They've always been in place and will always remain. If you have trouble visualizing *always*, I'd like you to imagine no beginning and no end. If the trouble persists, switch your imagination to an ant walking around a sphere.

The wandering ant reminded me of the luggage we'll take with us on our next trip. It will take some time to unpack it and start enjoying its benefits (or curses). Our new biological robes are rarely custom-made. You need to get used to it because at first it hurts and pinches here and there. Genes are different too, but spirit prevails over matter anyway, just as grass prevails over a rock. Although, when rains fail to sprinkle for a while, the grass withers and the rock doesn't care in the slightest. But we have a far greater primacy. If there's a drought, we can tap into a nearby river or dig a deep hole in the soil.

This doesn't change the fact that we have to deal with our biology. We have big heads and an even bigger mess inside them. Our limbs are flabby and temporarily of little use. Unlike, say, a horse—it can raise its head ten minutes after birth and stand up after an hour. But there's nothing to despair about, just couch your time quietly. In the end, you will mount it and not the other way around. After some time, the brain will also begin to work more efficiently, processing both new information and previously accumulated data. Then everything is up to you. When you roll a bum, you need to work much harder. When you roll five-of-a-kind, be careful not to be lulled into a false sense of security. Dive headfirst into new challenges. It's probably going to be light-heavy or heavy-light, in different percentage configurations. Most readers already know this anyway, so it's pointless to play a smart guy, dear author.

Chapter Twenty-Six

Humans differ from animals because we have access. That's why—provided we take advantage of it—we become skilled in abstract thinking and the use of imagination. This is how we were able to make friends with some animals back in the day. The aim was to eat them without bothering to hunt. We separated them from wildlife and neighbors, eliminating the threat of someone else eating them first. We also provided regular meals for the animal to fatten in peace. By eliminating mundane concerns from their lives, we also contributed to the degeneration of their natural instincts. However, this was of no serious consequences for them—they were about to be put under a knife or high voltage anyway.

But what would've happened if they were spared the inevitable fate of a schnitzel on a platter? Or a cut of beef for the broth? This was once tested on mice. Those nice rodents aren't on our menu? Not a big problem. They aren't particularly different from other four-legged creatures, so a tiny generalization is in order. You have no idea what experiment I'm talking about? I did ask you to acquaint yourself with the subject... never mind. A word of introduction to make your life easier: Several mice couples were locked up in a comfortable space, fenced off from the dangers of the outside world, with full board and health care. If the mice had any imagination, they would probably (at least some of them) smell their rat cousins and try to sneak out of the luxurious residence. Nothing like that happened. Abstract thinking wasn't exactly their strength.

I wonder, dear reader, if you could be lured by a similar offer. A luxurious villa. An unlimited line of credit to buy anything you want without ever having to pay back a cent. Gratis health care at the highest possible level. Free trips to any destination, with door-to-door shuttle and all-inclusive stays. So... would you sign up for the program? Be honest with yourself. The survey is anonymous, I'm not interested in the results; I won't share them with anyone. To make the decision easier, let me reveal the outcome of the mouse experiment. It ended in the total annihilation of the participating population. Without any outside interference, I might add. If you're curious about everything that transpired, read up on the details yourself, even if you don't like mildly displeasing yet very much educational stories.

I can imagine that some volunteers wouldn't be deterred even by that outcome, in line with the "Socialism yes! But without distortions!" principle (from time to time postulated in countries persistently experimenting with this lunacy). I'm not going to comment on that because I value my time just a bit too much. Let me only say that a theory is something that either works or it doesn't. This is the criterion of its usefulness, not good will or similar intentions. The latter are actually used in hell to pave roads, or so they say.

I have no idea about the intentions of the authors of the mouse experiment. I don't know what they were trying to study or whether they were surprised by the outcome. It's not relevant. They should be awarded the Nobel Prize anyway, and in all categories—the Academy would just need to bend the criteria accordingly. The details of the experiment should be put on the mandatory reading list in all schools, including Sunday schools, forestry schools, and even schools of fish, for all I care, so no one can claim they weren't warned. It should also be made clear that the outcome is always the same, no matter how hard everybody tries to prevent distortions.

And if you're annoyed with my constant reminders to put forth effort, you now know why I keep saying this. Admittedly, I'm doing this mostly for myself, but you can also heed the good advice.

One should be careful with offering others a paradise on Earth. This applies not only to the global saviors and their more or less whacky ideas. I'd recommend exercising caution with any support measures, even the small ones. Helping is a generally destructive act. That's how it works in Nature, whether you like it or not (some definitely don't). When you prop someone up, you usually make them weaker. But your self-love blossoms and you get your ego boost. Sometimes help can be useful though. This is the case when it goes to somebody who's willing to grapple with the vicissitudes of fate, does it (grappling) regularly, only occasionally asks for such help, and solidly justifies the request.

Let's take a farmer who isn't very wealthy. He lives in an unfavorable climate zone. Rarely he sees clouds in the sky, and if any, they're not always of the rainy kind. The farmer isn't discouraged though because there's a small lake a few miles from his field. He can get the water there, even though it's cumbersome and in the summer it often dries out. Such a fellow could be helped (as long as he asks for it), for example, by offering a non-refundable loan so that he can dig a well. Provided that his neighbors could also use the water (of course, only if they help with the digging). I recommend taking a closer look at that scenario if you're wealthy and want to allocate some of your surplus money to good causes. The best way to do this, in fact, is to find a farmer yourself. Well, unless you also want to support the brokers—along with their staff, rent, and representation costs.

"You mean, the weak shouldn't be helped?" I hear from the crowd, sensing the brewing outrage. "That sounds pretty naughty. The author propagates the law of the jungle! This is what sets us apart from animals—we care for our poor and give them a hand in trouble!" First, the law of the jungle, primeval forest, or any other heavily wooded area also applies in different locations: the meadow dotted with flowers, a brook meandering merrily among the fields, or a grove full of all kinds of birds chirping sweetly. Secondly, animal or human, the laws of Nature are the same for all. This is true even if some might not believe it, just because we are smarter and playing by different rules.

I have a friend with personal experience in institutional outreach. I can trust her opinion, unlike many others who know the area only in theory and never spent a moment working in the sector. She once told me a story about a group of people taking part in an outreach project, which supported them with foodstuffs once or twice a month. Over time, these people ceased to make any effort to get something to eat on their own. It's not that it was impossible—it only required facing problems and overcoming difficulties.

Of course I'm aware that this might be a very superficial analysis. After running comprehensive tests, one might have found out that all these people suffer from a certain syndrome or complex condition that prevents them from putting their heads down and working. This condition is rather incurable, but its symptoms can be alleviated. So the supplies should also include the appropriate medications. Since beggars can't be choosers, you could run a small experiment in the process. All for the common good, of course.

Just in case, let me mention that my skepticism regarding help doesn't extend to emergency situations. For example, when flames are engulfing a neighbor's property. Or when the ice has just cracked under someone. Or when my wife's friend is punched by a ruffian who turned out to be her husband. I also give money to buskers on the streets. However, I don't frame it as aid—it's but a modest gratification for the effort they put in, and the fact that they made my stroll around the city more pleasant. I don't support passive penny collectors, who just hold their caps or a plastic cup (which they empty out every once in a while). Sometimes they also tend to draw people's attention—verbally, with a true or false prayer, or a description of the problem scrawled on a piece of cardboard. No way. Just put some effort into learning to play any instrument. Even a comb. It's really not that difficult.

Chapter Twenty-Seven

I can imagine that my concept of Natural Reincarnation won't appeal to everyone. I call it mine because I've never heard of it before. It's certainly possible that somebody suggested something similar in the past. Perhaps even I did. If that's the case, I claim ignorance.

A slave trader would surely be skeptical of the idea of re-existence, being afraid of a nasty twist. In the next episode, he might be the one driven in shackles through the desert, or transported like an animal below the deck. Instead of being the flogger, he would be flogged himself. I also doubt that the judge of the Holy Inquisition would be enthusiastic about this concept. In his next life, he might become a heretic, which is a surefire way to go on a one-way trip to the lakeside with a stone attached to his neck. If by some miracle he managed to escape the predicament, it would only prove his dealings with the devil. And then he would end up like a sliced hot dog bun, or a hamburger boiled in oil.

In the present, when customs are a little less bloody, one still has to be aware of resentments. Celebrities, bathed in the splendor of glory, will be reluctant to swap the altar for a porch. Those who are strongly attached to their current complexion may not be fond of a new one. A teacher might not want to be a student again. A policeman might fear becoming a thief and vice versa. And a ruffian to change into a woman punched by her new husband.

The followers of different religions may also have their reservations. Where are the virgins at a young age and in large quantities? What about the guaranteed promotion for being faithful and devoted? Where is the immediate forgiveness of all misdeeds? By the way, I find it interesting that prayer can become a punishment. Looks like some kind of resocialization I don't quite understand. All of this, however, pales in comparison to a much bigger threat. What if fate, or rather the dice, roll the wrong way? And a new environment, even if in good faith, poisons the mind with false faith? Then what? Break the egg at the wrong end?

The idea of multiple existence (or rather singular, but in various settings) may raise other concerns as well. Someone might conclude that it supports suicide. It's an understandable act, after all, to cease suffering when the present life seems unbearable while the next one is at hand and new opportunities abound. Wait a second! Who said you won't get a bum again? What then? Another hop off the bridge? And the next one, until you roll something better? Let me remind you that your old baggage can't be thrown away. Or accidentally left on the platform. The great reset doesn't work, it's just revolutionary delusions. We all know how they end—always in big shit. Our bridge jumper (or whatever form of taking has been chosen) keeps carrying the same goods in his suitcases.

A new hand isn't going to change much in that regard, even if you do manage to get five sixes. You won't get rid of the stench. The shit won't dry out, either. You will have to open your baggage anyway and deal with both, whether in the slums or a five-star all-inclusive hotel. In fact, the stench will be worse off at the hotel. So there's no reason to postpone the fight—it's only going to get worse. If you're hungover or have the bends, you can work through the discomfort. I know it's hard, but after a day or two, or even more, everything goes back to normal. You can also take shortcuts. Just pour yourself another drink, or take another hit. It's exciting again, fast and effortless. You don't feel it yet, but another hangover is already on its way. Much worse than the previous one.

The various saviors and other social engineers won't be thrilled by my idea either. How to design a common happiness when everyone mainly cares about themselves? That is, unless you can persuade some people (preferably a lot of them) to give up on their own growth because it's rude to be so selfish. Especially since development is a thankless and tedious job. You need to make decisions on your own, consider problems, weigh pros and cons, learn stuff, get informed here and there. Still, you will make mistakes because to err is human. Then you'll have to deal with the consequences—usually unpleasant ones. And we (the saviors) know better because we've thought about this for a long time, read thick books, listened to distinguished professors, and participated in heated debates. So the wisdom overwhelms, not to say, overflows us.

Who should I count on then, I might ask, but I won't. If you're an attentive reader, you probably remember who the book's addressee is. And I'm not planning to establish any ideological, religious, social, political, or civic organization. Nor am I going to launch any foundation, corporation, institute, hotbed, or think tank. I don't care for clusters, groups, or bunches… unless it's about grapes, in which case I might be tempted to grab one. If you like the idea, feel free to use it in your life: in present and any subsequent, in parts or as a whole. There's no license, no fees, no warranty periods, and no terms and conditions. But also no answers for FAQs.

The only restrictions concern intermediaries and brokers. I'm not authorizing anyone, either in the near future or in a more distant one, no matter what certificates they produce to support their claim. All fees and commissions are also illegal in case somebody gets the wrong idea to make a few bucks on occasion. The message is simple and doesn't require any elaboration or interpretation as to what the author did or didn't mean. Everyone is free to come up with their own explanation. If you err in your way or go astray, Nature will remind you that you need to change course. The same goes for me, should I ever write or spout nonsense here and there. This is the only way to grow, and the possibilities are endless.

I restrict intermediaries, translators (except for different languages), or other interpreters because history knows many such cases where simple ideas have been zealously distorted, changed, or supplemented by various more or less noble-hearted visionaries and improvers. Who knows if today, after a solid facelift, the originators would be able to join in the ranks of their own followers. We have a full range of tools at our disposal. We have intellect, reason, common sense, instinct, intuition, experience. In general, we know what to do and how. When in doubt, we should make an effort and seek out knowledge. We don't need advisers who will tell us how to live, stand, sit, or lie down.

Or breathe, for that matter. Yes, dear reader, don't rub your eyes—you've read that correctly. It turns out that this seemingly natural activity has degraded over time. We don't really know how to properly inhale or exhale; or at least this was pointed out by some experts concerned with our condition. I can't help but see some contradiction here. We're supposedly so smart yet we tend to destroy everything we lay our hands on. Perhaps there's no contradiction after all. We aren't born equal, and not everyone is actually smart. Fortunately, some are. They probably breathe the way they should and will happily teach the oxygen-deprived masses to save them from extinction—at a reasonable rate, of course. Or maybe they'll come up with a clever device that will help us suck in enough air.

I'm a distrustful and inquisitive person, which is why I'm going to take a closer look at the breathing problem—just in case—so I can already start setting some funds aside for the future assistant. For starters, I'm going to rule out self-induced asphyxiation. I don't see the point of it, unless it leads to visions or hallucinations, but I'm not an expert on that either. In line with my dedication to research integrity, I tried it on myself by submerging my head in the bathtub for an extended period of time. I can't report any pleasant experience. Maybe the water was too cold? I also assume that the authors aren't a group of comedians (or maybe they are?), and that their conclusions are not an excerpt from a skit.

That leaves us with three options. The first is that the processes in Nature don't fix developmental bugs and we've been breathing poorly for a long time. That would mean that apes might be in trouble, too. We should check them and then go down the evolutionary

Chapter Twenty-Seven

ladder. Next, we'll have to fix the mistakes with the help of many people and lots of equipment, so huge funding is necessary. The second option is hardly optimistic. Only people have forgotten how to use oxygen properly, which means we're a failure and won't last long. There's also a third option, namely that the authors of these conclusions are simply spouting nonsense. And this is the option I consider to be the most likely after thinking about it for a while. So I'll take a chance and buy a new bike—without assistance, of course. If I get any change, I might add a skipping rope to the cart. A simple one will be enough—I can count the number of jumps myself, the clock is on the wall, and the calories... I'm taking care of that.

Part VII

WHAT ELSE?

Chapter Twenty-Eight

The representatives of the species *Homo sapiens* are at the very beginning of their developmental journey. No wonder everything is more or less still in its infancy. Some groups leaped ahead a bit. Others follow at a more moderate or even leisurely pace. Which hardly matters anyway. Everything will be verified at some point, and if someone decided to rush and accidentally went too far, they would have to retreat, maybe even as far back as the starting point. My ancestor Albert suggested that World War IV would be fought with clubs. Who knows, perhaps he was right.

Even if still in early infancy, there is one area in which we have achieved true excellence. By *we* I mean all humans, regardless of their pace, latitude, altitude above sea level, or even their salinity. This competence is making up stories. The term is used on purpose, equivalent to fairy tales and fables, to highlight the fact that they have little to do with reality. Inventors usually disagree.

Of course, I'm not talking about literary fiction. Its authors, also known as writers, openly admit (in some cases they are quite adamant) that their stories are solely products of their vivid imagination. By the way, I think that the term "writer" is vague at best and somewhat dismissive as well. It merely indicates the ability to put words on paper. What about the plots, dialogues, or colorful descriptions of lush nature? Where are psychological portraits, veiled morals, guilty consciences, and tarnished reputations? What about the various meters and exquisite (or even blank) verses?

Some writers have even gone a step further. They've created a form explicitly called a "fairy tale," aimed mainly at children. I have to admit—smart move! They tapped into a fairly large market. Little people often get gifts; givers are also available in abundance. In addition to the parents, there are grandparents (often two sets of them), all sorts of cousins and friends, not to forget godparents. Would they deprive a child of an interesting story that fosters imagination and provides enjoyment? Under the guise of fairy tale, the authors could also peddle their morals with impunity, regardless of whether the intended recipient was the beloved king or the common folk. At the same time, they didn't have to risk the wrath and revenge of either. "Calm down! It was just a fairy tale, bro!"

The Danish master of children's stories, Hans Christian Andersen, used an extremely interesting narrative device in one of his fables. It tells the story of two clever men who came up with their own fairy tale. The aim was to acquire a certain amount of cash without much effort associated with the entire operation. Lack of effort related to the process of acquiring. Coming up with the tale could even be quite absorbing. Their story was so absurd it seemed unlikely that anyone would fall for it. Nevertheless, they managed to achieve resounding success. The only hitch in their plan was a child, who decided to call out the nonsense.

I have no idea whether it was a premeditated action or just an accident. In any case, what Andersen managed to pull off there was quite astounding. He wrote a fairy tale for children in which the adults are either crooks or a bunch of nitwits (or rather dimwitted opportunists), and only a child cultivates honesty and reason. So reading it to the offspring requires a modicum of courage. Which is still better than your kids finding it on their own in some library and then doing an in-depth critical analysis. If anyone doesn't recognize the story, try finding it yourself. You'll stimulate your own growth in the process. And the writer, like the authors of the mouse experiment, should have been awarded the Nobel Prize. Especially given that the esteemed jury is right there around the corner. The story should be another compulsory school reading, primarily in the younger grades—not to promote the virtues but as a warning of how easy it is to lose them over time.

In addition to literary, there is also fictional fiction. I use this name because its authors deny that they make up stuff. This form is practiced by people on a massive scale, professionally and as a hobby, on every possible occasion. There are two main streams of this genre. The representatives of the first one surmise and often know very well that they are spouting crap or obviously lying. Others, for various reasons, are sanctimoniously convinced of the credibility of their fairy tales. This makes it impossible to question their good intentions. At most you can accuse them of stupidity, naïveté, or both. These two streams sometimes intermingle, and then it can get hard to figure out in which one the author is currently wading.

The vast majority of us, more or less consciously, tell fairy tales and stories. The question of whether this is a good custom is likely to be rejected by the same majority—it's kind of intuitive. And then we add to ourselves: "This isn't about me." Which will probably be another fairy tale. An obvious lie has an even more negative connotation. But what would life be like without our beloved scholars, who usually know better? Of course, this case is no different—as it turns out, you actually *should* lie. To avoid paying lip service, I'm going to present several quotes from an article. I'll skip the source and the name of the author out of indulgence, although I'm unsure if I'm flouting any rules here. But I don't think anyone in their right mind would want to fight in court to glorify a false statement.

"The ability to lie (...) is a valid sign of a flourishing spirit." "Teaching children to lie improves their performance on measures of executive functioning and theory of mind." Let me clarify—these quotes aren't from the inmates of a mental hospital but from those who sent them there. So if someone's confused and considering visiting a specialist, I'd recommend a moment of reflection. Besides, these quotes aren't taken out of context. I despise manipulation and don't use such techniques.

"Our society, our culture, the stability of this system is based largely on lies." Yet another quote from some learned psychopath. One of the readers of the article referred to it this way: "Given the choice between the stability of a society based on lies, I choose my own sense of happiness based on truth." I took the liberty of borrowing this thought because it perfectly captures my point. I doubt I'd be able to put it in such perfect words. However, it may be that the author of the commentary is slightly impaired. Another scientific virtuoso proclaims: "Intelligent people lie, the less intelligent tell the truth." Well, sign me up to the latter group then! Seems like I have a lot of work to do because the requirements are demanding.

The quotes above are the quintessence of the fictional fiction—telling stories about telling stories. In reality, it's a perfect example of what stupidity, lack of restraint, and arrogance can lead to when left unchecked. It's obvious that in some situations babbling isn't the thing to do. Sometimes it's even preferable to keep your mouth shut, according to the wise comparison to precious bullion. However, let's not twist everything around. Just because the vast majority of people practice something with joy isn't an affirmation of this activity. Just think of the slave markets or the centuries of mutual slaughter.

It's pointless to delve into scholarly explanations to evaluate a lie. Most of us, once it happens, hardly feel any particular satisfaction about it. I even daresay that the opposite is the case. If this sounds odd to you, I'd suggest an urgent checking of the fuses. I can imagine not everyone paid attention in physics classes. Perhaps some of you preferred spending that time in other ways, for example going to the cinema, playing soccer, or skipping rope. Or perhaps you were the type to take part in an oddball interest club. So let me explain: a fuse is a small and simple device that prevents a major crash once there's a malfunction in the system. Of course, this is true only if the fuse works.

Why do people invent stuff? Because they have the ability to do so. We gained access to a whole new territory with an infinite wealth of resources. But beware: when you cross the threshold of the new area and have the freedom to wallow in this wealth, you can't be too cautious, prudent, or moderate—it's very easy to overindulge (or just choke on it). For a better visualization I recommend a fairy tale. An actual one, this time, written by two brothers who were true experts in the genre. It's about an extremely rich, corrupt, and profligate sea creature (but everything has its limits), a greedy woman, and her henpecked husband who was in a fishing business. As always, you'll need to find the title on your own—no need to thank me for stimulating you to do some effort.

So, dear reader, you have access to limitless resources. You also have free will and the ability to make a choice. Will you invent a story, or can you resist the temptation? But the shortcut is so alluring. There is a chance to shine, at home or at a party; to flatter your own ego or do it for someone else; to take advantage of people—they were asking for it; to ridicule an opponent—because he's a crook; to destroy your competition—they were unfair, so who cares. It might even work for a while. But eventually everything gets verified, and then there's no "sorry" or "I didn't mean to do that!" Although changing course is always possible. Well, almost always.

Besides the story about the benefits of lying, one of my personal favorites is another tale about the origin of humankind and the reasons why we managed to get so far ahead of the other quadrupeds, bipeds, and nopeds. (I include in the last group fish, snakes, and earthworms.) There are many versions of this fairy tale (I leave out the wizard using the magic touch option). They all share the same original sin, which asserts that the incredible development of the humans and our dominance over other species is the result of random chance. Try to solve a very long and complicated mathematical equation that starts with the assumption that $2 + 2 = 5$. The end result will always be wrong no matter how hard you tighten, flex, or strain.

Another sin—perhaps of a lower caliber, but still grave enough—is the habitual confusing of causes and effects (or the other way around, whichever you prefer). The idea that humans started to develop language because they had brains that were big enough for it is a prime example of such confusion, which is based on previous confusions. Humans had bigger brains because they started eating meat (jeez, what would the vegetarians say!). They started enjoying meat because they came down from a tree. (I thought they actually fell out of it by accident.) People developed verbal communication because they felt the need to say something more. Let me list a few names: Homer, Dante, Shakespeare, Goethe, Pushkin. Their predecessors came to the conclusion that it would be difficult to achieve this goal using the old methods of communication, like chirping, grumbling, and even roaring. So they decided to make an effort. This resulted in the gradual development of an apparatus suitable for speaking, along with the evolution of the brain (no matter what they ate during the lunch breaks).

Before anyone tries to twist things around: people didn't develop speech to strengthen social ties because it was better due to evolutionary reasons. Other species do very well without being able to converse or even make small talk. Unless we are also just animals, and the only goal is to dominate others. If so, we've obviously achieved great success—there's nobody out there who can kick our butts. Well, maybe except those small creatures, which you can't even see (and guess what, they can't talk either)—they do still bother us a little. But that's because of their insidious nature and pitiful size. Apart from that, it all adds up. If you're happy being a great ape, only a talking one—sometimes wisely, sometimes like a fool—all the power to you.

I'm not going to bring up any more fairy tales, even though there are many—a nearly endless supply, really. Rounding them all up and selecting the most important ones would be enough to keep a group of people divided into several teams and sub-departments busy for years to come. In the meantime, more stories will pop up, and they'll also need to be catalogued. But I'd like to inspire the disappointed readers with some words of encouragement. Perhaps I'll go ahead and write another book just about them? Or prepare an anthology spanning multiple volumes with alphabetical and thematic subdivisions? To make things easier and to ensure a better variety, you too, dear reader, could submit some of your stories. Anonymously, of course—no need to feel embarrassed or ashamed!

Chapter Twenty-Eight

"Well, that sounds great, dear Author, but what about your own story?" I hear some of the most sharp-witted readers ask. Right, here we go. (And thanks for calling me an Author with a capital A.) "What if this book is just another fairy tale? Huh? Making fun of others only to spin your own fantasies scot-free— that's just poor form." I would reply that everyone has a mind and that nothing prevents you from making up your own. Are my suggestions true? I think so, and that's it. I'm not eager to convince anybody, just myself. Others can do whatever they want. The license is free and valid indefinitely; you can use it or... not. As for me, I'm trying to avoid telling stories. Well, with the exception of true fairy tales, preferably read to a child at bedtime. Actually, I wrote one myself.

Chapter Twenty-Nine

Beyond the seven mountains—or valleys, depending on whether you counted the bulges or depressions in the terrain—a rumor began to spread among the people that something was wrong. No one knew exactly what was going on. Some said there were strange spots on the sun, but perhaps it was a rash. Others mentioned space dust turning into gas, or the other way around. Still others spoke about field reversal and related changes in the polarity. What they couldn't work out was whether they occurred before or after the field was reversed, and which—or whose—field it was all about.

Gradually, more and more information came to light, and after some time it became clear—when the specialized experts took the matter into their hands, or rather under the microscopes—that the situation was actually serious. They discovered that a new, previously unknown, and very mysterious radiation had emerged, which was harmful and therefore dangerous. The hitherto somewhat lethargic media, or rather people working there, who at first completely underestimated the informational potential of the events and, in their shortsightedness, never assumed there might have been even a small plague going on, started reporting on it—first with some reserve, and then more and more vigorously—

turning things up a notch (as they always do) so that the product sells better.

The public, at first more amused than concerned, began to exhibit a hint of nervousness over time. Some recalled a cinematic production on a similar subject that had been shown in theaters earlier that year, showing a lot of people who suffered rather gruesome deaths. Though just a movie, it was extremely well done, winning awards for the screenplay and special effects. Some speculated that it may have been based on secret facts, and that all the mentions were quietly cut out. To make matters worse, the weather was perfect, and the lack of clouds reportedly facilitated the spread of the contagious radiation. Unfortunately, although everyone would usually be happy about it, long-term forecasts suggested that the weather would remain good for some time to come.

Shortly after, there was news of the first casualties with rather unpleasant descriptions. They were almost always struck without warning, and the symptoms bore a deceptive resemblance to those usually observed in panic attacks, only they refused to subside. It was mostly shortness of breath, coupled with the agonizing feeling of choking, as if someone was crushing your chest with a sack of cement or had tightened a band of steel, known as a hose clamp, around your throat. Convulsions, paresthesia, and derealization were also mentioned, as well as frequent non-systemic dizziness, fainting, and various losses of consciousness. While consuming horror reports from the media—and these went like hotcakes—it started getting stuffy and not only for the victims. Plague aside, an overwhelming fear began to creep over people as well.

It became even more overwhelming when it turned out that, once irradiated, the victims would also emit the insidious rays themselves. As a result, they posed a real threat to others without knowing it. At least that was what experts claimed after having spent some time studying the issue at hand. This information somewhat saddened the rulers of a certain powerful state, who didn't have the reputation of being particular friends of civil liberties. But they did care about their subjects, so they didn't hesitate to act quickly and decisively. They chose a large city where the clouds had been in short supply recently and decided to lock it down. No one could enter or leave; movement inside was severely restricted as well. This was needed in order to isolate the plague and nip it in the bud. Some suggested that the authorities used this opportunity to practice the sealing off of major metropolitan areas in preparation for future unrest due to various reasons, but perhaps this wasn't the case and the officials had simply panicked.

As the media was already alert and the topic hot, chilling images circulated around the world, showing that the fun was over. Armored vehicles covered with a special reflective film slowly rolled down the deserted streets. The officers, clad in spacesuits and helmets, which were the only clothing that could protect against the harmful rays, scanned every precinct and district, locating outbreaks of the plague and its possible victims. There weren't many of them —the vast majority of the terrified residents hunkered down in their houses anyway, sealing the cracks in windows and frames with whatever they could find at hand. People in other regions followed the reports with flushed cheeks, while anxiously glancing at the constantly cloudless sky. Most still hoped that the worst would miss them or at least pass sideways, although the sweaty forehead and increasing pressure in the chest didn't bode well.

Eventually both waves, radiation and fear, one more powerful than the other (or perhaps the other way around), spilled over the dams and started to take their toll. Those overcome by panic and unable to withstand the pressure, stormed local healthcare facilities, where equally fearful yet heroic staff did their best to prevent the worst. The howling sirens of the ambulances reverberated through the empty streets, further adding to the apocalyptic impression. In a desperate attempt, the suffocating were hooked up to devices designed to help them breathe, which they did—mostly with fatal outcomes. Someone suggested that maybe this isn't the way to go, but you're not supposed to say "no" when every life matters.

Despite the danger, brave journalists ventured inside the hospitals to report from the front lines, showing overcrowding, medics collapsing due to tiredness, and the languishing patients, covered with all kinds of tubes and hoses. The most popular, however, were the pictures of coffins, either stored or transported here and there. According to the principle of supply and demand, this material was served up the most frequently, usually accompanied with suitably dramatic commentary, further ramping up the panic. And the commercials played in the meantime reached exorbitant prices. It was the only entertainment available anyway, as cinemas, theaters, restaurants, as well as laundries, beauticians, and barbers were all shut down.

Sensing the mood of the population, the authorities encouraged people to stay home, and seeing the great support, decided to order them to. More and more countries closed their borders to prevent foreigners from importing the plague. Police in riot gear patrolled the streets, fighting with homeless people who had no media receivers and thus weren't aware of the situation. They had no idea that they were supposed to hide, and it wasn't like they had anywhere to go, either. Specialist experts who normally received rather scant attention and were overshadowed by their peers from climate, overpopulation, and racial prejudice, started enjoying their newfound popularity and the increasing media attention. Some, dazzled by the glow of the spotlight, offered wild theories and similar advice on how to counteract the misfortune.

According to them, bald people were the most at risk, followed by those with bends and thinning at the top. This boosted the demand for wigs, hairpieces, and all kinds of toupees, even for the owners of a lush mop of hair. Some resorted to animal products, shearing rams on a massive scale or hunting beavers and ermines. But it was only the discovery that swimming caps provide the best protection, and the regulation to wear them compulsory not only in the pool but everywhere else without exception, including when sleeping (or even taking a short nap), that made most people feel a little safer. Later, some researchers discovered that umbrellas worked even better, especially the transparent ones, which covered the head down to the shoulders. Soon after, they too were mandated, along with double swimming caps. By contrast, all types of buckets, bowls, and barrels, even those with punctured eye holes, were classified ineffective.

All of this of course didn't mean that the danger had been averted. Quite the contrary. Although in the meantime the weather had turned, and it rained heavily from the dark clouds, the clever rays managed to learn how to navigate under them, resorting to reflections and going back into outer space. In addition, the tireless experts found that they are extremely cunning, constantly changing the intensity of their beams, which made locating them nigh impossible. As if that weren't enough, they attacked people from behind corners and without warning, in such a perfidious way that the attacks often went unnoticed. Fortunately, thanks to the heroic efforts and around-the-clock shift work, special dosimeters were developed and quickly deployed to the market so that people could see who fell victim to the rays and who didn't. Only then did the full extent of the tragedy become apparent, so people were ordered to stay at home and not set a foot outside except in the case of urgent needs. The authorities kept checking whether the people would buy it; as it turned out, they lapped it up with glee.

Some groups of civil liberties defenders protested here and there, accusing governments of having trampled on democracy and of having authoritarian inclinations—confusing in the process freedom with the power of the people, who are not always interested in the former, especially when they are shit-scared. The public response was therefore rather tepid, and the troublemakers were publicly disavowed, albeit only slightly, as they posed no real threat —unlike the deadly radiation. But there was a light at the end of the tunnel in the form of a special life-saving liquid that could be sprayed on people in special shower stalls. The potion formed a protective layer on the skin, impenetrable to the enemy. In addition, it wasn't washable, especially if the baths were repeated from time to time.

In this way, the plague was defeated, and the human mind triumphed once again. The helpless rays kept attacking every once in a while to no avail, until finally they realized that it was of no use, so they went irritated from whence they came... or to another place. People breathed a sigh of relief and resumed their daily business, although some were a bit sad, as it's not often that you live through exciting times. Experts were also a little frustrated because the spotlights went out, and the cameras were turned toward other objects that weren't as attractive, but alas—no El Dorado lasts forever. And let this be the moral of the tale. If you're disappointed because you expected a stronger one, feel free to draw it on your own.

Chapter Thirty

Does the idea of colonizing Mars, and perhaps other planets, make any sense? In my humble opinion, not at all. This, of course, doesn't apply to business ventures. If there are people willing to take a ride into space, or spend a vacation on some near or distant celestial body, who, in addition to the mere desire, have the necessary financial resources and the willingness to use them for this purpose, the providers will appear as well and overcome any associated difficulties, no matter how complex they may be. All thanks to the all-pervasive principle of supply and demand. The same is true of other services, such as hair styling, hooking, or bungee jumping, although these don't require as complex logistics and advanced technology.

I'm skeptical about projects with broader scopes—things along the lines of a mass migration—that various visionaries consider inevitable if we dream of surviving as a species. To make this a reality, however, we need a suitable location. If we start running away blindly, we may find our doom even faster. To my great relief, I recently read that some savior actually managed to pinpoint the right place. It's still in our solar system, so not even that far away. I think it was about the two moons of something, which means we could viably separate people with different worldviews. With the necessary modifications and improvements, such as installing artificial gravity and devices that destroy or perhaps only repel asteroids that roam the space and threaten to collide, it would apparently be quite nice there.

I wonder where the visionary got the funds for his epochal discovery. If it wasn't private money, his own or someone else's, the local populace should probably take a closer look at how their ruling representatives are spending the collected tax revenues. As for neutralizing the boulders floating in outer space, I'd suggest deploying the appropriate tech somewhere around Earth. This would be a much simpler and cheaper solution, especially since it looks like we don't need extra gravity. The remaining funds could be used to give access to running water here and there (it would be more than enough for both here and there), make it potable, and add sewer systems to boot.

There are many more areas where things could still be improved, repaired, or simply cleaned up here on Earth, so perhaps there's no reason to get ready for the cosmic trip. We didn't fall from the sky. We are the result of natural developmental processes that have been taking place on Earth for an awful lot of years. Keeping in mind how Nature works, with its relentless verification and heavily enforced standards, we've survived a lot. The prospects for the future aren't too bad either. I therefore suggest we exercise the necessary moderation and curb some exuberant fantasies.

This can be useful regardless of the activity. René Descartes—for movie lovers he is perhaps better known by his nickname Cartesius (if you still have no idea who I'm talking about, feel free to look him up, it's not going to be too hard)—said and wrote many wise things. But he delved so deep in his contemplations, or even embroiled, not to say embrangled, that he reduced humans to their mere thoughts—since our senses are imperfect and tend to deceive us. This is an undoubtedly profound, or at least quite interesting, observation. However, its practical application in everyday life may prove cumbersome. Some might say that philosophers aren't for practical advices but for philosophizing, to which I say, by all means, but a bit of restraint never hurt anybody.

This very valuable tip doesn't apply only to the aforementioned Cartesius. It would also be useful for other representatives of his profession, who explore the mysteries of human existence and related topics. I have to admit that despite a lot of perseverance and numerous attempts, I haven't been able to familiarize myself more thoroughly with any of their teachings. It was always due to the same reason—sooner or later, I stopped being able to comprehend what it was all about. In fact, I wouldn't rule out that the authors themselves had a similar problem, only they were too embarrassed to admit it.

Regardless of curiosity, the word *why* shouldn't be overused. Why? Because it can be done indefinitely. There's no final answer, and if someone insists that there is, it's a clear path to frustration or, God forbid, depression. Even small children know this. Sometimes they fake an excessive thirst for knowledge by persistently repeating the magic adverb (alternatively interjection, noun, conjunction, or relative pronoun). In reality, they're just checking on whether they can trust the addressee, at whose mercy they have been left. If the test is negative, they start crying out of fear.

You can go overboard because you were given this opportunity. You have access to immeasurable resources and the freedom to choose whether and how to use them. As a result, you're able to create things and conditions—an arsenal of extraordinary firepower. I'm just not sure if you realize what that actually means in practice and what you'll be confronted with. In the other corner is Nature, with its perfect and inexorable rules that work always and flawlessly. All it would take to get knocked down is some straight or cross, while dropping the guard for a moment. Sometimes, this might result in a KO.

It's worth keeping one important thing in mind. I'd even say a very important one, perhaps the most important of all. I haven't touched on this topic thus far, waiting for a convenient moment, but enough is enough; we're probably not going to get a better one. In addition to development, harmony is another key category for Nature, which means the right tuning of all components, their balance, proportions, and the like. Harmony is the control criterion.

Chapter Thirty

The level of its advancement determines the outcome of the verification of existing structures and the status quo. If the inspection reveals an inadequate degree, a correction shall be made—tiny, bigger, or complete.

About this harmony, it's not some kind of a seminal discovery, or an extraordinarily bold conclusion. As always, all you need to do to see it for yourself is carefully observe the surrounding reality, both past and present. (You can also try looking into the future, but even there nothing will fundamentally change.) Everything, small or large, near or far, is in a kind of correlation and interaction with its surroundings—and in some harmony. When the harmony is weak, adjustments are common to change it. If the whole thing works well together, the system becomes more stable and resistant to crash tests or other adversity. This applies both to the place where we live in the Universe and to the small group of people who are commonly referred to as "family." The components and scale are different, but the principle remains the same.

We can brilliantly describe harmony using music as an example. There are a few ingredients, the rules are simple, and the result is immediately available to everyone. (Well, maybe not to everyone, but there's no reason for deaf people to despair, because it's only temporary.) Sound is the noise that something makes when it bounces back and forth: usually a piece of metal, wood, leather, or air, sometimes a combination. Harmony in music is the interplay of sounds. They can appear one after another or several at a time. Then a few others, together or separately. These appearances are not completely random. They're caused by a human being, one or more, sometimes a whole bunch of them, which is then called an orchestra. If there are even more people, the orchestra is joined by a choir—presumably a four-part mixed one.

When music sounds cool, it's not due to the height or the handsomeness of the composer but because of the way he put the notes together. If the harmony is right, the ears will confirm it. You don't need any special knowledge—just listen. Sometimes you might feel tears of joy or sadness, your heart might skip a beat, or you feel a sudden urge to rush to the barricades. A miserable set of sounds might only evoke an indifferent shrug at best, more likely irritation followed by the desire to forget it quickly. This tendency intensifies when harmony is completely neglected and replaced by hubbub. I commend this to the attention of today's followers of Bach, Mozart, and Mahler, should they consider how to avoid obscurity and oblivion.

On this occasion I'd like to mention that, for example, a violin can produce noble and beautiful sounds. This was once ensured by gentlemen like Stradivari, Amati, and Guarneri, as well as their less famous colleagues. If you write music and plan to limit your work to rasping, squeaking, and crackling, you might want to consider using alternative instruments. A washboard, a mortar, and a comb would probably be more suitable for this purpose. The sound effect will be similar, perhaps even better, and virtuosity can be achieved in a much shorter time.

Any innovator, radical, or revolutionary, as well as a fat man who just wants to significantly reduce his body weight, should remember that moderation is key. Before and after. Every change disturbs the existing harmony, making it unstable and prone to disintegration. The more disturbed it is, the more unstable it gets, or vice versa. And it likes to return to the equilibrium because it knows this condition and worked hard to make it all somehow fit together (which is well known to anybody who's ever tried any miracle diets). So, I'd recommend going step by step, and the steps don't have to be big at all. They shouldn't be. Especially since there's no rush. We're still only 0.2% of the way in.

Chapter Thirty-One

Tell me, dear reader, did you perhaps get the impression that I don't have any particular esteem for scholars and researchers? If so... your intuition didn't fail you. Let me highlight that my emotional restraint doesn't pertain to the activity itself. It stems only from the status that the learned comrades get to enjoy these days. Not that I care about it that much. All deviations are doomed to the same end—the dumpster or the recycling plant. At its peak, however, the trend can be somewhat cumbersome, and overcoming artificial difficulties is simply a waste of time. Even if you have a lot of it. On the other hand, any problem, including a pointless one, stimulates your development in some way. I'm not sure anymore: should I be sad or happy?

There have always been people in the world who were curious. Unlike their more passive colleagues, they couldn't find inner peace and persistently tried to explore the ins and outs of everything, or to unravel this or that mystery. It probably started with some kind of an observation, like why a kicked stone first moves and then stops. Maybe they even tried to present the dilemma at a tribal meeting. We may assume that the response was poor. Their colleagues focused rather on effectively defending themselves against neighbors or how to attack them successfully.

Being perhaps of lighter stature, and thus less useful for fighting or hunting, the inquisitives had plenty of time to indulge in their favorite activity, which was searching for answers. In the process, they stepped into uncharted lands. This forced them to act innovatively—how else would they get to the secrets? They conducted various experiments, the nature of which is that you don't know how they end. Of course, you can always assume a thing or two, but it doesn't have to go the way you wish. I'd even say it often doesn't go this way. The result is mostly surprising, but such is the nature of the business. If you don't like it, go fight or hunt instead.

So there were a lot of defeats and many fewer successes. From time to time an arm fell off, someone went blind or deaf, or they bid farewell to life altogether (sometimes the experimenter, other times a random witness). No wonder it was easy to fall into disfavor and the activity was generally regarded as suspicious—which was by all means the right approach, in spite of the passion and dedication of the researchers. When you enter a minefield, you can't blame others watching on skeptically. And no insurance company would issue a policy for it.

The fact that the inquisitives err is perfectly normal. The odds are never really in their favor. This was the case a long time ago, a little and much later, recently and today, and that's how it will remain in the future. The researchers themselves might find it hard to swallow, but most of their work isn't worth much. However, we should keep in mind that without this work, the important things would often not appear. So there's no reason to make fun of past researchers and their views. Today's scholars are going to face a similar assessment. Arming themselves with more or less curved glasses and entrusting data analysis to powerful computers won't do anything to help them. Machines don't think, so they can't shoulder any of the blame.

A large portion of distrust and far-reaching suspicion should be part of a daily routine. And constantly oppress researchers. These days, however, we've been experiencing the erosion of these very useful mechanisms for harassing them. In fact, we are dealing with the exact opposite—it's learned fellows who tyrannize the rest. All because one haze replaced the other. From the very beginning, people felt that they had stepped into something very serious. They couldn't quite put their finger on it, so they were relieved to hear their brethren claiming that they know. The knowledge was about how everything is guided by some powerful beings, who were reduced over time to just one with an entourage. If you follow their preferences—those who knew had somehow managed to get familiar with them—you'll be able to get along reasonably well. Now and in the future.

Apart from the knowers, there was yet another group, like kings, sultans, or other chieftains. They were responsible for more earthly affairs and the day-to-day business. Eventually, these two groups formed a well-functioning symbiosis that flourished for a long time. The content changed, of course, and there were tensions or disagreements, but the collaboration continued without any major disruptions. Meanwhile, the inquisitives tinkered around with this and that. They rigged up some boulder thrower or a Trojan horse, poisoned someone on demand, invented a nifty torture device—all to satisfy the needs of one or the other leading class. They themselves were an insignificant group with little influence and a poor reputation.

Which got even worse when they started rummaging in the skies. This was an area reserved exclusively for the knowers. They weren't stupid and knew well about the weak spots. They quickly noticed the danger and decided to act—either by burning the inquisitives' works, or the authors themselves. But it was all in vain, and the situation began to spiral out of control. As time went on, the powers that be also started changing their optics. And the subjects, a little bored with the same narrative for centuries, were increasingly eager to lend an ear to new ones.

Sensing favorable conditions, the inquisitives picked up steam and went on the global offensive. They announced that the existence of divine-almighty beings is somewhat doubtful. Or rather, they don't exist at all. And the knowers are nothing but conmen messing about with people's heads. We (the inquisitives) have been inquisitive for a long time and now know better. Henceforth, we are the knowers, and the former are just the confusers. But that wasn't the end of it. Why would it be? Hell doesn't exist anymore, so who cares? They concluded that instead of wandering about in the hereafter, we can build a paradise here on Earth. After all, we're already very smart... or at least some of us are. The heavier work will be done by machines. Artificial intelligence will do the thinking. We'll live longer and longer, ultimately even forever because we'll grow spare parts. And for different ailments, you could always inject the right concoction.

That sounds really impressive. Of course, this or that killjoy could bring up mice, their earthly paradise, and the sad finale of the experiment. But hey, there's always one—perhaps a secret agent of the former elite? "Now we have a new one that will lead us toward a bright future!" Well, I wouldn't overdo it with this *new* thing. People don't change that much, whether they're wearing a black cassock or white coat. Every revolution—October, French, or scientific—likes to use the tried-and-tested models of the overthrown opponents. The convoluted language, for example, works very well in that regard. If you don't understand it, show respect to those that do.

I once sat in a pub, sipping on a beer. The patrons at the neighboring table were sharing their impressions of a concert that took place as part of a renowned festival for contemporary music. The residents of this not-so-large city are very proud to host an event of such international standing. My neighbors admitted quite frankly that they couldn't understand and appreciate what they'd just heard because they hadn't reached the appropriate level yet. I'm not kidding; that was the gist of it, although the words might have been different. I wanted to say something—for example, that music isn't meant to be understood but to be listened to. I wanted to bring up Andersen and the tale of the weavers... I changed my mind. I didn't want to spoil their evening.

It wasn't only the intricate language that had been adopted by the new elite. If something isn't intersubjectively verifiable, it's deemed to be false. You don't understand what I'm talking about? It only confirms your low status. That's how it is classified by new

Chapter Thirty-One

knowers who look at things cumulatively and progressively. Just like the Holy Inquisition used to decide whether you blasphemed and spread heresy. Scientists—that's what the new knowers are called now—also know better. How come? It's because they use scientific methods to derive scientific hypotheses that they confirm with scientific studies that are reviewed by the scientific community in scientific journals. Amen, you might be tempted to whisper spontaneously, but it's the wrong century, so you'd better bite your tongue.

Exploring the secret matters that can't be grasped by the human mind also worked excellently for the previous elite. So the cat that's simultaneously alive and dead fits like a glove. This is why any quantum business is welcome because nobody knows what's going on, and that's the point. If they ever run out of it, there are still white dwarfs torn apart by black holes. Which reminds me of Prometheus and the vulture feeding on his entrails (or an eagle, depending on the version—it doesn't matter much for the feeding itself). I have to admit, I kind of like the dwarf that's torn apart better, but it's a matter of taste, of course.

Scientists aren't dealing with anything mysterious. They're trying to understand how the reality around us works, what it consists of, and what processes take place therein. There's nothing wrong with that interest. It's similar to when inquisitive children, usually boys, destroy their favorite excavator to see why the light comes on when they press a button. There are times, however, where the researchers go too far guided by their curiosity. They start splitting hairs, then splitting the resulting pieces and the next resulting pieces of the previously split. They do it because there are too many of them. Researchers, not hairs. Everyone wants to have something to do. Fortunately (for the researchers), you can split indefinitely.

In addition to observing and trying to understand, scientists also deal with improving things. Tinkering is the domain of researchers with more practical inclinations. Every once in a while, we get something useful out of it. Let me remind you of the wheel, water pipes, or electricity. This even applies to the atomic bomb—

its live presentation dampened the enthusiasm for war in large parts of the Earth's population.

Scientists interested in consumption are more likely to poke at plants or animals. Minor corrections, such as a seedless watermelon or a pig that gives multiple hams, are (somewhat) acceptable. After all, we're multiplying on a massive scale, and people have to eat. Perhaps it doesn't taste as good as a deer or wild boar that you've killed yourself, but you don't have to chase through the woods. And you can go to a supermarket to get all kinds of spices to fix the flavor, anyway.

Scientists dealing with people face a real challenge. A human being is an extremely defective commodity that really needs to be thoroughly overhauled. We can't even handle basic physiological functions. I've already mentioned our inept attempts at breathing. It's a miracle we haven't collectively suffocated yet. Our nutrition is downright scary at times. We eat harmful foods prepared in even more harmful ways. Don't get me started on sleeping, not to mention standing, sitting, and even lying down. We don't walk enough, and when we do, we're going the wrong way. There's hardly an area, at least not among those studied by specialists, where we're doing well. Something tells me that this trend will only increase after more research. It may come as a bit of surprise that, despite our poor performance, we somehow live longer and longer, but this is rather a lucky coincidence, and we're going to run out of good fortune relatively soon.

Scientists and experts are our only hope. I suppose they've identified and eliminated all the human infirmities in their own bodies first and are now ready to help their fellow men as well. Another question is whether there's enough time for help. Their colleagues who specialize in wide-ranging issues claim that we are emitting too much. It's going to have a rather terrifying outcome—some kind of global flood or equally global drought. Most likely both in the same place and at the same time. Like in a Greek theater, no less. This realization should give us some encouragement—perhaps all is not lost yet? After all, there's one area in which we've achieved unsurpassed mastery (see chapter twenty-eight).

Chapter Thirty-Two

When you break an arm—it can also be a leg or a rib—apart from being in trouble, you also feel a nagging pain from the broken bone. It's truly intriguing why Nature gives us additionally such an unpleasant sensation. Not only is the bone damaged and the patient less functional, but you also suffer on top of that. As a sign of empathy, or at least compensation for the damage suffered, the injury could be signaled, say, with a gentle warmth or a pleasant tingling. This would soothe the frayed nerves and improve the currently miserable mood. Why the extra punishment while we're already down?

That's a good question. Why do we need pain? I keep asking this in conversation with my family and friends. Usually, I get one of two answers. Some say that pain informs us about an imminent danger, as evidenced by the increasing discomfort when you get your hand closer and closer to a flame or some other source of heat. It might also be a signal that something's wrong, most likely at the exact site of pain, which should prompt the sufferer to see a doctor. Unfortunately, I have to conclude that both of these theories are false.

If we had an early warning system, it would work for other threats as well. Imagine somebody taking hold of a nail—small or large, it doesn't matter (it can even be rusty, for all I care). He then puts it next to the kneecap of another person he doesn't like very much (he tied that person to a chair earlier). To get a better feeling of the situation, let's assume that you're the victim. The reason behind the perpetrator's lack of sympathy is a certain amount of money you should've paid back some time ago, but you didn't. In the other hand the aggressor holds a massive hammer. The expression on his face shows that he's serious about driving a nail into your kneecap. He even raises his hand upward (the one he's holding the hammer in). Now the contact point between the nail and the kneecap should start to hurt a little. You could even indicate it, hoping for mercy and maybe for stopping the punching process. Yet there's no pain. (Of course, the nail has to touch the skin very softly, but that's the case because the perpetrator is holding it carefully.) So why is it that when you bring your hand closer to the embers you feel pain, but when you see a swinging hammer, you only get a little nervous?

The same happens when you stroll barefoot on the beach and suddenly a shard of glass gets embedded in your sole. It used to constitute a part of a bottle previously containing a high-proof alcoholic beverage consumed the night before by some thirsty beachgoer. Upon discovering that the flask is already empty, he became a little frustrated and smashed it against a nearby rock. Just before your foot comes into contact with the glass, when the step has just been taken and the touch is unavoidable, an alarm should be triggered. Some painful or at least unpleasant impulse. Nothing like this happens. A moment later, cursing loudly, you try to relieve the stabbing pain while soaking up the blood oozing from the punctured artery. Let me ask again: Why didn't the system warn you this time either?

A hammer gliding through the air or a glass shard protruding from the sand don't cause any damage. This is going to change quickly, but then it's too late. With a flame, embers, or an electric stove burner that have just been switched off (already dark, but still very hot) the situation is quite different. Heat is just the particles of matter in motion. The faster the motion, the greater the heat. Such rapid movement can cause destruction of more delicate structures that happen to enter the area where this motion is taking place. It won't affect a stone, but human or even buffalo skin for certain (although the latter a bit later).

Let's assume you're getting your hand closer to the flame. This should normally be avoided, but it's frosty outside, and your manus is stiff. Its surface begins to be damaged by particles of heated air hurry-scurrying around. At this point, you start to feel an unpleasant sensation. Not because it's going to get even more so—which is bound to happen if you don't pull your hand back or, worse yet, bring it even closer. The damage is already done, although the extent is still limited. It works in a similar fashion the other way around. So it's a good idea to cool the burned area immediately. All you need is cold tap water, or better still a stiff sausage from the freezer. The movement slows, and further destruction is avoided.

It hurts when something gets injured or doesn't work the way it should, whether for a moment or in the long term. This causes a signal to be sent to the control panel so your organism can do something about the problem. The signal can't be enjoyable—otherwise there would be no reaction, other than the desire to maintain the status quo. Only pain stimulates the system to act. And most people to visit the doctor, although that was hardly the point. Pain as an unpleasant sensation evolved long before the first doctor came to be and wasn't dedicated to him. The signal is meant for us to carry out corrective action, without the involvement of any third parties. The only problem is—we don't want to wait. Nor do we intend to put up with the discomfort associated with the signal. This is understandable, although a little more confidence in the abilities of one's own body wouldn't hurt at all.

I checked it empirically once. I was jogging along the riverside when suddenly I started feeling pain in that damn calf again (never mind which one, what does it matter?) A few weeks earlier, a similar problem cut my run short and forced me to walk back home. It didn't put me in the best of moods because the problem occurred near the spot where I turn around—right, in the most distant point from the start and finish line. So I limped away, wasting a lot of time and cursing my shoddy muscle. I also learned that I would have to forgo my morning runs for a while, until the muscular tissue in question returned to a reasonable state. In order to avoid being grounded again, I decided to push my limits this time. I went on, ignoring the sharp stabbing in my lower leg. After some time, it gradually began to subside. If you want to repeat the experiment, I'll be honest with you—up to that point the pain was rather unbearable. Interestingly enough, I haven't felt the same pain since, contrary to the gloomy predictions of a physician friend with many years of experience.

So the potential seems reasonably high. Do you bathe from time to time, dear reader? I don't mean the tub (we're not that close). I'm thinking about larger reservoirs, like pool, river, or ocean. The water should be cooler than your body temperature, so hot springs and geysers are out of the question. If the answer is "yes," then you know what I'm talking about. After a certain amount of time you have to get out of the water to relieve your bladder. This happens much faster than if you stay on the shore in the first place. Although —excluding pools (and even here there are exceptions)—you don't really have to get out. Fish and other aquatic creatures don't go anywhere to relieve themselves. You either get out or not, and after a while you start feeling the same urge again. This also happens without water if you're accidentally locked up in a cooler for storing beef or turkey carcasses.

Whether in water or a cooler, you pee more often. At the moment it's better to get rid of excess liquid than to waste energy on keeping it at the right temperature. It will come in handy in more important areas also affected by cooling. Your body knows this. It makes its *own* decisions, usually the right ones (if they are wrong, maybe just don't interfere too much). They are the result of years of experience and testing, checking every possibility and constantly verifying the outcomes. Excessive peeing is just one of the hundreds, thousands, or an awful lot of actions and activities that our system performs constantly. What's more, they all lead to improvements (or degeneration, depending on the body's owner).

We are well equipped to deal with a biological world. You might even say we couldn't get any better. After all, we're at the top of the evolutionary chain. Nevertheless, we keep going to the doctor. It turns out that things aren't so rosy at all. A variety of diseases are lurking around, and they're very cunning; they attack without warning. Some remain in hiding, waiting for an opportunity to strike. They can keep their heads down low for years because they are persistent and patient. Only doctors can deal with them. They're the ones who discovered all the diseases, and there are thousands of them. (I mean the illnesses; docs can be counted in millions.) Besides, new ones are constantly being found, so there shouldn't be a shortage of work in this field either.

Our own defense troops are unlikely to do anything. For reasons known only to them, they often act like a bunch of deranged pyromaniacs who inflame things here and there. Fortunately, brave firefighters in white scrubs nip all the outbreaks in the bud. Otherwise, some people could go up in smoke for good. It's all a bit puzzling. Our body has an awful lot of years of experience gained in the toughest fights and battles. It knows all too well what to do. I dare say, it knows best. Why give up this knowledge? I think I'm beginning to guess the secret. The anti-inflammatory drug that suppresses the body's natural response is simply an invention out of this world, a divine elixir to say the least. It's referred to as a medicine, by the way. Which suggests that it fights the disease. Which further suggests that the disease is self-inflicted. Which would indicate suicidal or at least masochistic tendencies.

Unless the strategy is more sophisticated. We disrupt natural reactions to make fighting off the enemy more difficult on purpose. This should strengthen the entire system and boost its efficiency—an exceptionally clever approach. However, something tells me that it's not the case. I'd rather pick minimizing the customer's discomfort, even at the cost of delays and lower efficiency. The same applies to pain management. In essence, we are blocking the nerve connections that carry the unpleasant stimuli. This could be compared to shooting at an ambulance rushing a patient to the hospital, the siren wailing, with a rocket launcher. Its owner couldn't stand the noise and decided to free himself from it.

Thankfully, the shooter missed the target. Quite a relief, given that the ambulance was carrying an inattentive carpenter and his hand, which had been cut off a little earlier by a circular saw. The hand was put on ice; the carpenter wasn't. Should the ambulance get to the hospital in time, clever doctors will even try to sew the hand back on. This kind of medical intervention is perfectly legitimate, just like helping someone run over by a streetcar, kicked by a horse, or stabbed by an annoyed neighbor. In the case of a stomach disorder, tonsillitis, or even ear pain (which can be quite bothersome indeed), I would suggest exercising some restraint before seeking professional help. Your system has already started the rescue operation. You can help it by remaining horizontal for a little while. Eating a cup of hot broth won't hurt either. In case of a temporary lack of appetite, which is understandable in this situation, water will suffice. This simple liquid is a much better choice than any cure—whether purchased from a nearby pharmacy or prepared by a local herbalist.

Some people might consider my suggestions rather eccentric. Well, there's something to it. I don't know many people who'd follow my advice. It requires patience, training, and accepting more or less temporary discomfort. In addition, you can't be afraid. You should be utterly convinced that you can do it. Otherwise, it's not going to work. As always, I only intend to convince myself, although I may not have to. I'm currently practicing this method without any outside inspiration. Nobody persuaded or cleverly indoctrinated me to give it a shot. Perhaps the future me will also know that or be able to come to this conclusion intuitively, who knows? I'll leave that mention here just in case. You never know what kind of company you will end up with in your next run.

"Thanks to medical advances, people are living much longer," say friends, who are troubled by my carefree attitudes to health—simultaneously regurgitating popular belief. Well, I'll be honest with you: I don't yearn to be immortal. The older you get, the less fit you are, sometimes even infirm. As is the case with everything, it's important to exercise moderation. The road is long, and there are many journeys yet to come. As for medical services, they are just one factor when it comes to our lifespans (I dare say, not even the most important one). I'd wager that it's a matter of better hygiene—meaning water and sewage systems, an abundance of food (even if genetically modified), less exhausting work done in more bearable conditions, as there are more and more machines. Let me add one thing—this all comes without any side effects.

Chapter Thirty-Three

You probably know foosball—a pub game that mimics a soccer match. We also sometimes refer to it as table soccer because it's played on a table, rather than in a stadium. The table has several rods with the figurines of players attached to them. Each team uses four rods—they control, counting from the goal (your own, of course, otherwise the order is exactly in reverse), the single goalkeeper, two defenders, five midfielders, and three forwards. I wonder why they decided to go with this formation, which would be unthinkable in a real game of soccer. Well, there's one possibility —a poorly paid coach, trying out innovative tactics in order to throw a game and cash out a bet against his own team.

The different formations perform various movements, always fully synchronized. They move to the right or left (of course from their perspective because the player pushes them away or pulls them closer). Sometimes they bow. This is not a sign of courtesy—usually it's followed by a violent movement in the opposite direction, which often turns into rotation, commonly called spinning, and this is against the rules. They can also kick the ball. In fact, only one player does, and the rest just imitate the movement, probably to confuse the opponent. If you think about it for longer than a second, you will conclude that this isn't a fair assessment. Due to the design limitations, they simply have no other option. Unlike, say, synchronized swimmers who could swim on their own, but stick together at all costs.

Real-life soccer players are also divided into groups, but they aren't attached to anything, not even tied together by an ordinary rope. They have much more freedom and are happy to use it. They're part of the team, but each of the players tries to accomplish their own goals on the pitch—dribbling past the opponent, passing to a guy wearing a similar shirt, tripping the guy wearing a different shirt, diving to convince the referee that it was the other guy who tripped him, eventually putting the ball in the net, preferably the opponent's one, otherwise there is an own goal (but of a different kind). All the claims of doing this for the team are just a sham, although it can't be ruled out that some players believe it. If that were the case, they would play for their beloved club regardless of how much money they make, without haggling over every pound or dollar only to change their colors at the sight of an extra portion of mammon.

The same is true for every group: small, large, or even humungous. What matters are the interests of the individual. When you go to a family gathering, you're happy (or not at all) to have the opportunity to see other family members, not because they can see you. When you put your hands on the person who desires you, you satisfy your own lust, even if your partner enjoys it as well. If the cumulative effect is positive, this is called a collective benefit. The same happens when a team wins a home game and then ties the rematch. The club is promoted to the next stage and earns extra money. Of course, the owners get the biggest slice, but individual players profit as well, only less. And the fans have their own personal joy, even if they celebrate as a group.

There's no such thing as collective interest. There is only the sum of individual interests. If they happen to overlap to some extent —in the case of a soccer team, most likely to a very large one— everyone rejoices and it's all fine and dandy. The same is true of social, national, regional, continental, or even global interests. When you live in a group, you have to coordinate your own desires with those of others (at least to some extent, because everybody takes care of their own stuff anyway). Alternatively, you can move to a sparsely populated area—or, following the example of a certain Robinson, to a place with no population at all. Then you won't have to make arrangements or take anyone's preferences into account. There's also no possibility of talking to anybody. Unless the island turns out to be not-quite-deserted and a native or castaway would be happy to learn a foreign language.

Politicians, even the noble-hearted ones, who are few and far between, typically talk about the common good and making every effort to help the collective. In most cases, this is pure crap spouted out of ignorance, stupidity, or as a calculated tactic. Usually it's the latter. Besides, promising pies in the sky, they don't differ that much from the rest. Perhaps the level of hypocrisy is a little greater, but this should actually be listed in the job description. The manufacturers of laundry detergents are also lying through their teeth. Just watch their ads—they present a yellowed garment that turns snow-white when removed from the washing machine. Despite the fact that it never seems to work like that at home, many hypnotized people buy their products anyway. We also readily lie to ourselves. We solemnly promise that we're going to do it... tomorrow, for sure! Well, the day after tomorrow at the latest! And then we hardly care at all, but there's always some important reason for that.

The stories told by politicians hardly discourage their prospective voters. They usually pick the ones who look better and can handle public speaking. Nobody does a thorough content analysis anyway. The same applies to the possibilities of implementation. After the plebiscite is over, everybody goes home and minds their own business. That doesn't stop them from criticizing their elected officials shortly afterward, calling them "bastards" and claiming that they only have their own interests at heart. Excuse me, but why should it be any other way? And they're not always bastards; their interests may be quite diverse. After satisfying personal ambitions,

Chapter Thirty-Three

some might want to do things to benefit others, be it by building a park with squirrels, getting clean tap water to the city, or creating a pedestrian zone without exhaust fumes.

The constant whining about politicians is a popular pastime. After all, it's easy to blame others for one's own misery. If you ever get bored with it, I have a solution that will make such whining pointless (or at least highly questionable). The scheme relates to elections and the management of large structures. With the necessary adjustments, it can also be adapted to smaller communities.

Let the legislators be directly elected by the citizens every couple of years—voting for political parties, committees or individual candidates. Whatever works best. "But this changes nothing, we're already doing that!" you contend. Well, that's true—at least if your country's relatively free, and there is political competition. The new part is a representative power, also to be elected for a limited term by means of a popular vote. I'm referring to a president, chairman, or some other father or mother of the nation who is eager for prestige and honors. Alternatively, this function may also be exercised by an existing monarch of any sex, if that is what the local populace would prefer. Judges who can serve until old age, unless deemed unfit for duty, will be appointed by the president or king—let them have something serious to do after all.

The executives should have no ties to the legislature. They should be selected by means of competition. The candidates, who would have to meet a list of initial criteria, including prior political abstinence, should pass a battery of tests and then answer many difficult and tricky questions, all controlled by impartial machines. The seats would only go to the best—for a fixed period of course, and independent of the length of the legislative term. They would receive some amazing salaries, so only elites would apply. They should be held accountable for wrong decisions, including jail time and the confiscation of assets if they go too far overboard. In addition, a balanced budget with no debt. At most, a tiny surplus in case of a volcano or another tsunami.

The executives should only implement the law and not create it.

They should also be able to get rid of weak legislation if they believe that it would bring more harm than good or if it cannot be meaningfully implemented. And the lawmakers who've signed off on crap laws a third time would be barred from further terms. This should effectively motivate them to strive for quality, as well as curb their creativity to a reasonable scale. Government representatives would be tasked with doing the work and managing things efficiently, without having to give a damn whether the citizens like them or not. Meanwhile, the monarch or president would visit the victims of floods or earthquakes, as well as attend important sport games played by the national team, expressing all kinds of solidarity platitudes, because they would have to take care of their good image among the subjects and the masses.

Of course, the details need to be ironed out. It will also come out in the wash what should be improved or corrected. But I think the direction is right. I also think that no one is going to seriously consider this option for a long while. I shall therefore continue to cultivate my voting abstinence. Should the need ever arise, I'll change the location to one with a lot of freedom. If there's a shortage of these places, I'll use a map to find an area with a lower population density.

So... the collective interests. Do they exist or not? If it were up to voters to decide, the majority would check "yes"—especially if the poll wasn't anonymous. They would select this option mainly out of fear of negative feedback from their fellow humans, as well as being dubbed a selfish egoist. This hardly changes the fact that the vast majority of people enthusiastically pursue nothing but their own personal interests (which is good and normal, otherwise we wouldn't exist anymore). Yet, at the same time, this isn't considered a virtuous trait. Most people have no idea what to say when asked about it, so they just go with the flow. Judging from what it's like to be on a river—in a canoe, swimming, or even wading through shallow waters—this is an easier way.

Staunch advocates for the common good confuse it with compromise. They aren't into any independent effort or toil. They tend to prefer unified models and collective bliss—the prelude to the mouse experiment. We know the outcome. So everyone needs to make a personal decision about what to do with this. Fortunately, unlike mice, we are capable of abstract thinking... well, at least some of us. We also have free will, this time without any exceptions. Although not everyone is entirely convinced that we do.

Chapter Thirty-Four

Some time ago I had the opportunity to watch a speech by a well-known and respected thinker. The topic was free will. The speaker gave the impression of a highly intelligent man. He managed to outline his thoughts in a clear and precise manner. He spoke with conviction and passion, yet very calmly. There was also no shortage of humorous elements, neatly highlighting the above-average erudition of the speaker. The form had reached the highest level. The content, by contrast, was nothing but a load of rubbish. I'm not using this unpleasant expression to criticize the author's views, which roughly boiled down to the belief that free will is an illusion. Everybody has the right to hold their own opinions, but discrediting them with derogatory terms is poor form. I lowered the level in regard to the arguments presented by the speaker to support his views.

One of them was an experiment that featured the pressing of green and red buttons. The esteemed speaker claimed that by the time we choose one or the other, our brain had already made the decision. Let me not question the order right now, however problematic it may be. That would mean that I and the main organ of my body, which controls all its processes, are two separate entities. My grey cells don't quite belong to me, while the hand that pushes the buttons does—to follow the author's perceptive reasoning. What about my liver, spleen, and appendix? Do my eyeballs belong to me or not? Not to mention the auricle, nails, and calloused epidermis. I believe that as a matter of scientific integrity there's an urgent need to clarify these issues.

Analyzing who I am as a person—while applying the usual dose of sense and common intuition—I had little trouble defining myself in a reasonably meaningful way. That's how it was up until now. It turns out, though, that the *self* is some highly abstract concept. In my simplicity, I'm unable to properly understand its meaning. Irony aside, this is what false assumptions, ideological bias, overintensive education, and excessively persistent goal-seeking lead to, especially when one wants to make an impression.

"Free will is an absurdity—you never know what you're going to think about or say in a moment." Well, dear speaker, sometimes you could think about whether you should even refrain from talking for a while. The wise lecture contained many more such revealing thoughts. I don't want to go into them, much less write about them, because words fail me. Okay, I might mention just one more—with a particularly twisted message. A psychopathic murderer isn't guilty of his actions. His penchant for killing others stems from his miserable genes, pathological parents, and the kind of environment he was exposed to when he was young. This implies specific chemical reactions and electrical impulses occurring in his body. There is nothing the psychopath in question can do about it, even if he really wanted to. He's destined to commit evil deeds, like a poorly programmed automaton, just because he lost the birth lottery.

The same goes for a rather significant group of people from a certain country in the middle of Europe. In the first half of the twentieth century, they decided to wipe out another group of people whom they didn't like too much. I write "significant" because it's impossible to kill millions if you don't have tens or hundreds of thousands of active collaborators involved in the process. They had to be perfectly aware of what they were taking part in, although later down the line many of them developed memory problems. What happened to these psychopaths afterward? Did the chemical reactions in their brains, compelling them to perform inglorious acts (which they could do nothing about, obviously), suddenly stop occurring, as if by an act of magic? Hint—if we switch the order and start believing that my brain is me, the issue doesn't look as mysterious anymore. And the aforementioned group, the one who did the annihilating, wasn't particularly terrible compared to people in other countries. All they had was a penchant for efficiency, whether it was manufacturing cars or sending people to the hereafter.

I believe that the speaker was misguided. Which is not to say that I don't understand his arguments. Let's assume for a moment that a human being is just a more literate animal. This animal is nothing more than a collection of tiny particles of matter, subject to certain chemical reactions (slightly more complicated than in the case of stone, but that's the only difference). Suggesting free will suddenly feels like the ramblings of a madman. If the author believes that he is merely an advanced version of the dolphin, or a machine without its own will and powered by chemistry and electric impulses, his argument is completely justified. We could only be sad about the direction in which the fauna on our planet is evolving.

Animals of one species hunt down selected representatives of another in order to eat them. The motivation isn't antipathy but a growling stomach. They rarely eat their own kind. I heard that bigger fish in an aquarium can consume the offspring, but I have no idea if they also go for their own. But the reason is quite similar—to satisfy hunger. People kill other people because they don't like them. (Oh, sorry, they are driven by electrical impulses.) Let me pull up the data from the twentieth century, starting with the birth of a certain noble man, also known as an advocate of a rather amicable conflict resolution; it was a century that was quite civilized compared to the barbaric customs of the past. In this time, the internal chemical reactions of the successors of the octopus, parrot, and chimpanzee, to name some of the leaders of the animal intellectual elite, wiped out several hundred million people. I'm talking about wars and revolutions, which are collective affairs. I'm not counting personal disagreements with fatal consequences.

That sounds sad, but we are seeing a serious genetic degradation. Has anybody ever seen hordes of wolves killing each other? One herd of zebras trampling another one? Packs of sparrows and chickadees pecking their own kind to death? Thankfully, the scientific avant-garde noticed the problem. They already started hinting —still timidly, but let's not lose faith—at the need to make some adjustments to the human genotype, as well as other visionary experiments related to rummaging through the secret nooks and crannies of our degenerated organisms. One can only hope that those who run these ambitious projects are not deformed themselves. I shudder to think what other new duds could come out of a faulty machine.

Free will is what sets us apart from the animals—as well as the plants, fungi, and bacteria, let me go down the evolutionary ladder. I'm not going to mention the objects without any vital signs. Free will is the essence of being human. Just like the ability to replicate is the essence of biological life (the ability to evolve is the essence of both). And chemical reaction, dear speaker, is a method of implementation, not a cause. The car moves because its wheels go round. Why? Because the shaft turns. Why? Because there are various reactions in the engine, because a spark was made, because something caused the plug to spark. Why? Because I've turned my key in the ignition. Or pressed the start button if the vehicle in question is more sophisticated. This is assuming that I have a car in the first place (or enough money to rent one).

It's all about development, as is the case with everything in Nature. Only in humans does the process take place (or not) at a much higher level and with no apparent threat of serious consequences for those who are reluctant to participate. A rogue—if he's smart and doesn't cross the line—is going to be just fine as a living being. He won't be killed by a heart attack or some other stroke, at least not earlier than a very decent guy who might be a little hypersensitive. A lion that lets itself go needs to find a zebra in a similar condition—because it isn't going to catch anything else. And when the lion goes hungry it'll get weaker and turn into prey for a bunch of hyenas that (while the lion was letting itself go) focused on learning how to hunt efficiently. If a human villain lets himself go, he can still walk around on this Earth for a long time no matter how horrible he is. There's no threat of annihilation at first glance.

On the other hand, the possibilities are almost limitless. So we find ourselves in a difficult situation, but the trouble contributes to progress and development. The rest is up to each individual. Free will lets us decide whether we are going to evolve or rather abandon this arduous activity. To evolve as a human being, not as an animal, although physical fitness doesn't hurt at all. This was rightly pointed out some time ago by a certain Decimus Junius Juvenalis, who said, "*Mens sana in corpore sano*," because that was the only language he could speak. Free will is more than just the ability to choose between a grey and red binder, pick out which car to buy, decide whether you want to get a Mac or a PC, or vote for the Purple or the Yellow Party in the upcoming election. Machines would do that just fine and wouldn't have to be particularly complicated at all.

I'd suggest using free will in more serious situations. For example, by signaling to the emperor—despite the high risk of losing a well-paying job—that the guys who are making his new clothes are simply conmen. Even if they themselves and the various opportunists around the ruler suggest something completely different. Or by informing a greedy spouse—even if she's threatening divorce or at least to spoil the atmosphere on a long-term basis—that the trips to the fish are over. It's been very generous anyway and moderation is key. At worst, the possessive companion can be left behind. Which probably won't happen—she'll calm down when she sees what's going on.

Enough fairy tales. Everybody can figure out when to use free will. You can choose the direction, get the result, then experience the consequences. (Choosing the latter is impossible—they can be mitigated at most.) Then, another decision needs to be made. Then again. And again. It never ends, whether we like it or not. In the process, some people might get lost. Perhaps they were too lazy or made the wrong choice—several times and deliberately. Given the stringent standards, many will presumably be lost, but not by accident or unfairly. The rest, repeating the attempts, will use free will more and more efficiently. Practice makes perfect, as we all know.

That's it, dear reader. Third time's a charm, so now it's for real. Are you disappointed because you were hoping for even bigger revelations? Think of the fisherman's wife and the lamentable consequences of excessive desire. If you disagree with my ideas, try not to be sad or frustrated. The reality is what it is, regardless of beliefs and the degree of attachment. If you spare no effort in bettering yourself without harassing others and messing with their heads, you'll always come out on the plus side, regardless of what flag you wave in the process. Focus on yourself—it's always a valuable endeavor. Trust your own instincts and experience. Stop listening too much to those who tell you they have a solution to everything. Ignore the specialists of spreading fear. Treat other people with kindness. If you happen to meet a scoundrel, try to keep away from them rather than convert. Let me remind you once again—we have an awful lot of time. There's no need to rush or keep stressing about not getting there on time.

And then you can live really long. And pretty cool on top of that. *Bon voyages* (plural intentional), dear reader.

Made in the USA
Columbia, SC
30 March 2025